Vegan Bodybuilding Cookbook

100 Best Vegan Bodybuilding Recipes

By: Michael Beckett

Please Note

This book is a Language book. Copyright © 2019 by Dirk Alan Llorens. All rights reserved worldwide. No part of this publication may be reproduced or transmitted in any form without the prior written consent of the publisher. Limit of Liability/Disclaimer of Warranty: The publisher and author make no representations or warranties with respect to the accuracy or completeness of these contents and disclaim all warranties such as warranties of fitness for a particular purpose. The author or publisher is not liable for any damages whatsoever. The fact that an individual or organization is referred to in this document as a citation or source of information does not imply that the author or publisher endorses the information that the individual or organization provided.

Contents

Breakfast Recipes 7
   1. French Toast 8
   2. Tofu Scramble 10
   3. Avocado Toast 12
   4. Spinach Quiche 14
   5. Banana Bread 16
   6. Quinoa Porridge 18
   7. Banana Pancakes 20
   8. Beet and Hemp Granola 22
   9. Seed Cereal 25
   10. Germ and Berries Parfait 27
   11. Apple Pancakes 29
   12. Berry Beet Smoothie Bowl 32
   13. Chocolate Chia Seeds Pudding 34
   14. Gluten-Free Pancakes 36
   15. Carrot Cake Overnight Oats 39

Desserts 41
   1. Coffee Chia Pudding 42
   2. Protein Brownies 44
   3. Warm Blueberry Yogurt 47
   4. Pumpkin Spice Mug Cake 49
   5. Almond and Orange Creamsicle 52
   6. Date and Cashew Truffle 54
   7. Avocado Ice Cream 56
   8. Mocha Pops 59
   9. Frozen Strawberry Yogurt 62

10. Banana Maple Cookies 64
11. Coffee Avocado Pudding 67
12. Protein Fudge 69
13. Coconut Pumpkin Ice Cream 71
14. Protein Crepes 73
15. Pumpkin Pie Soft Serve 76

Lunch Recipes 78
1. Wild Rice Salad 79
2. Red Lentil Soup 82
3. Tomato Spelt Pasta 85
4. Chickpea Falafel 88
5. Alkaline Gravy 91
6. Quinoa with Acorn Squash 93
7. Tempeh Lettuce Wraps 96
8. Broccoli Salad 99
9. Quinoa Bites 101
10. Lentil Jamaican Curry 104
11. African Lentil Stew 107
12. Mexican Burgers 110
13. Quinoa Salad with Mango 113
14. Creamy Red Curry 116
15. Sweet Potato Tots 119
16. Tabbouleh Salad 122
17. White Bean Salad 125

Dinner Recipes 128
1. White Bean Gravy 129
2. Vegetable Biryani 132
3. Cauliflower Rice with Peas 135
4. Curried Vegetables 138

5. Teriyaki Tofu Burger 141
6. Coconut Cashew Rice 143
7. Black Bean Burger 145
8. Black Bean Soup 148
9. Buckwheat Salad 151
10. Thai Quinoa Salad 154
11. Waldorf Salad 157
12. Hearty Soup 160
13. Cream of Asparagus Soup 163
14. Greens Lentil Soup 165
15. Pumpkin Soup 168
16. Barbecue Tofu 170

Snacks 173
1. Protein Queso 174
2. Edamame Spinach Vegan Hummus 176
3. Peanut Butter Protein Bars 178
4. Chickpea Brownies 180
5. Keto Crackers 183
6. Baked Sweet Potato Shoestring................ 186
7. Fruit Salad 189
8. Candied Carrots.. 192
9. Plantains With Maple Syrup 195
10. Roasted Chickpeas 198
11. Trail Mix 200
12. Butter Bean Dip...................................... 202
13. Maple Glazed Pecans 204
14. Chickpea Cookie Dough 206
15. Roasted Edamame 208
16. Tofu Nuggets 210

Shakes and Smoothies 213
   1. Almond Banana Cream Shake...................214
   2. Coconut Cream Pie Protein Shake 217
   3. Blue Protein Smoothie................................219
   4. Coconut Strawberry Protein Smoothie......222
   5. Peanut Butter Green Smoothie 224
   6. Peanut Butter Protein Shake 226
   7. Red Juice 229
   8. Nut Smoothie...232
   9. Pineapple Pie Smoothie.............................234
   10. Orange Turmeric Smoothie 236
   11. Mango Lassi 239
   12. Strawberry Almond Protein Smoothie 241
   13. Banana Orange Smoothie 244
   14. Kiwi Smoothie...246
   15. Pumpkin Protein Smoothie.......................249
   16. Power Packed Smoothie 252
   17. Chia Lucuma Smoothie 254
   18. Tune Up Smoothie 257
   19. Mango Hemp Seed Smoothie 259
   20. Spirulina Smoothie 262
   21. Cashew Milkshake....................................264

Breakfast Recipes

1. French Toast

Serves: 1

Ingredients

- 6 oz. soy milk
- 2 tbsp flax meal
- 1 scoop vanilla lean protein
- 2 tsp vanilla extract
- 2 tsp cinnamon
- 2 slices gluten-free bread

Directions

1. In a baking dish, mix milk, flax meal, protein powder, vanilla extract, and cinnamon until well combined.

2. Now, dip the bread slices one by one in this mixture to coat well.

3. In a nonstick pan, cook the toast over medium heat for almost 2 minutes each side.

4. Garnish with your favorite berries, banana slices, and syrup. Serve and enjoy!

Nutrition Facts

Servings: 1

Amount per serving

Calories 386

	% Daily Value*
Total Fat 13g	17%
Saturated Fat 1.9g	9%
Cholesterol 135mg	45%
Sodium 193mg	8%
Total Carbohydrate 23.7g	9%
Dietary Fiber 5g	18%
Total Sugars 10.9g	
Protein 38.6g	
Vitamin D 0mcg	0%
Calcium 193mg	15%
Iron 2mg	10%
Potassium 466mg	10%

*The % Daily Value (DV) tells you how much a nutrient in a food serving contributes to a daily diet. 2,000 calorie a day is used for general nutrition advice.

2. Tofu Scramble

Serves: 1

Ingredients

½ block tofu, crumbled
30 grams of raw spinach
1 tbsp nutritional yeast
Salt and black pepper
1 tbsp of your favorite salsa

Directions

1. In a non-stick pan, over medium heat, add tofu and cook for almost 5 minutes. Keep stirring to prevent sticking.
2. Add yeast, spinach, salt, and pepper and cook until spinach is light green.
3. Serve hot after garnishing with your favorite salsa.

Nutrition Facts

Servings: 1

Amount per serving
Calories 79

	% Daily Value*
Total Fat 2.6g	3%
Saturated Fat 0.5g	2%
Cholesterol 0mg	0%
Sodium 131mg	6%
Total Carbohydrate 7.5g	3%
Dietary Fiber 3.9g	14%
Total Sugars 0.9g	
Protein 9.5g	
Vitamin D 0mcg	0%
Calcium 134mg	10%
Iron 4mg	20%
Potassium 524mg	11%

*The % Daily Value (DV) tells you how much a nutrient in a food serving contributes to a daily diet. 2,000 calorie a day is used for general nutrition advice.

3. Avocado Toast

Serves: 4

Ingredients

1 avocado
4 slices of whole grain toast
4 tablespoons of hemp seeds
4 tablespoons pomegranate arils
Salt and pepper to taste

Directions

1. Mash the avocado and put on the toasts.

2. Top with pomegranate, hemp seeds and sprinkle with salt and pepper. Enjoy.

Nutrition Facts

Servings: 4

Amount per serving

Calories   296

% Daily Value*

Total Fat 17.1g	**22%**
Saturated Fat 2.5g	**12%**
Cholesterol 0mg	**0%**
Sodium 129mg	**6%**
Total Carbohydrate 26.3g	**10%**
Dietary Fiber 9.1g	**33%**
Total Sugars 8.2g	
Protein 10g	
Vitamin D 0mcg	0%
Calcium 116mg	9%
Iron 4mg	20%
Potassium 384mg	8%

*The % Daily Value (DV) tells you how much a nutrient in a food serving contributes to a daily diet. 2,000 calorie a day is used for general nutrition advice.

4. Spinach Quiche

Serves: 4

Ingredients

- 1 unbaked pie crust
- ⅓ cup almond milk
- 1 cup soy cheese
- 1 scoop vanilla lean protein
- 8 oz tofu
- 10 oz spinach, thawed
- 1 tsp garlic, minced
- ¼ cup onion, diced
- Salt and pepper to taste

Directions

1. Preheat the oven to 360 F.
2. In a blender, blend tofu, protein powder, salt, and pepper, and milk and blend until smooth.

3. In a bowl, mix spinach, onions, garlic, tofu mixture, and soy cheese. Mix well and pour into the pie crust.

4. Bake in the oven for 25 minutes until golden.

Nutrition Facts

Servings: 4

Amount per serving

Calories 338

% Daily Value*

Total Fat 20.3g	**26%**
Saturated Fat 7.2g	**36%**
Cholesterol 34mg	**11%**
Sodium 369mg	**16%**
Total Carbohydrate 23.7g	**9%**
Dietary Fiber 3g	**11%**
Total Sugars 3.7g	
Protein 16.6g	
Vitamin D 0mcg	0%
Calcium 229mg	18%
Iron 4mg	22%
Potassium 615mg	13%

*The % Daily Value (DV) tells you how much a nutrient in a food serving contributes to a daily diet. 2,000 calorie a day is used for general nutrition advice.

5. Banana Bread

Serves: 6

Ingredients

2 cups gluten-free baking flour
2 tbsp olive oil
1 scoop vanilla protein powder
4 tbsp potato starch
6 bananas, mashed
1 tsp baking powder
3 tbsp maple syrup
½ cup brown sugar
Salt to taste

Directions

1. Preheat the oven to 360 F and oil the baking pan.
2. In a bowl, mix flour, baking powder, vanilla powder, and salt.
3. In another bowl, mix olive oil and sugar; stir well. Also mix in potato starch, bananas, and maple syrup until well blended.

4. Mix this mixture with the flour mixture and stir well.
5. Pour the mixture in baking pan and bake in the oven for 25 minutes until baked.

Nutrition Facts

Servings: 6

Amount per serving
Calories   401

% Daily Value*

Total Fat 5.9g	8%
Saturated Fat 0.8g	4%
Cholesterol 2mg	1%
Sodium 16mg	1%
Total Carbohydrate 82.2g	30%
Dietary Fiber 7.1g	25%
Total Sugars 32.3g	
Protein 9.1g	
Vitamin D 0mcg	0%
Calcium 125mg	10%
Iron 1mg	4%
Potassium 551mg	12%

*The % Daily Value (DV) tells you how much a nutrient in a food serving contributes to a daily diet. 2,000 calorie a day is used for general nutrition advice.

6. Quinoa Porridge

Serves: 4

Ingredients

½ cup quinoa
2 tbsp of brown sugar
1 ½ cup almond milk
¼ tsp cinnamon, ground
1 tsp vanilla extract
1 scoop of protein powder
Pinch of salt

Directions

1. In a heated pan, add quinoa over medium heat and season with cinnamon. Cook for 5 minutes.
2. Add milk, vanilla, protein powder, salt, some water, and brown sugar. Mix well.

3. Cook and bring to a boil, then simmer for 30 minutes. Stir often.
4. Serve and enjoy.

Nutrition Facts

Servings: 4

Amount per serving

Calories 336

% Daily Value*

Total Fat 23.2g	**30%**
Saturated Fat 19.4g	**97%**
Cholesterol 16mg	**5%**
Sodium 69mg	**3%**
Total Carbohydrate 24.2g	**9%**
Dietary Fiber 3.5g	**13%**
Total Sugars 7.7g	
Protein 10.6g	
Vitamin D 0mcg	0%
Calcium 55mg	4%
Iron 3mg	15%
Potassium 408mg	9%

*The % Daily Value (DV) tells you how much a nutrient in a food serving contributes to a daily diet. 2,000 calorie a day is used for general nutrition advice.

7. Banana Pancakes

Serves: 1

Ingredients

2 bananas
4 tbsp coconut flakes
½ scoop protein powder
Cinnamon powder

Directions

1. Mash bananas in a bowl with the help of a fork until smooth.
2. Now, add cinnamon and protein powder and stir well.
3. Make pancakes from this mixture and leave the pancakes in sunlight for 1 hour. After an hour, flip the sides and leave for another hour. Serve and enjoy!

Nutrition Facts

Servings: 1

Amount per serving

Calories 341

% Daily Value*

Total Fat 8.4g	11%
Saturated Fat 6.6g	33%
Cholesterol 32mg	11%
Sodium 34mg	1%
Total Carbohydrate 58.8g	21%
Dietary Fiber 7.9g	28%
Total Sugars 30.6g	
Protein 14.3g	
Vitamin D 0mcg	0%
Calcium 62mg	5%
Iron 4mg	21%
Potassium 1004mg	21%

*The % Daily Value (DV) tells you how much a nutrient in a food serving contributes to a daily diet. 2,000 calorie a day is used for general nutrition advice.

8. Beet and Hemp Granola

Serves: 6

Ingredients

- 1 tbsp coconut oil
- 1 cup rolled oats, soaked
- 6 medjool dates
- 1 beet, steamed
- ½ cup hemp seeds
- ½ cup sunflower seeds
- ⅓ cup golden berries
- 1 tsp cinnamon, ground
- ½ cup of water
- Salt to taste

Directions

1. In a blender, blend the dates, beet, cinnamon, water, and salt. Blend until smooth.

2. In a bowl, mix the oats, seeds, golden berries, and dates mixture. Stir well.
3. Line a baking sheet and spread the mixture over it smoothly.
4. In a dehydrator, dehydrate it for almost 8 hours at 120 C. Serve with almond milk and berries.

Nutrition Facts

Servings: 6

Amount per serving
Calories 300

% Daily Value*

Total Fat 12g	15%
Saturated Fat 2.7g	13%
Cholesterol 0mg	0%
Sodium 25mg	1%
Total Carbohydrate 44.9g	16%
Dietary Fiber 6g	21%
Total Sugars 29.1g	
Protein 9g	

Vitamin D 0mcg	0%
Calcium 48mg	4%
Iron 3mg	17%
Potassium 463mg	10%

*The % Daily Value (DV) tells you how much a nutrient in a food serving contributes to a daily diet. 2,000 calorie a day is used for general nutrition advice.

9. Seed Cereal

Serves: 1

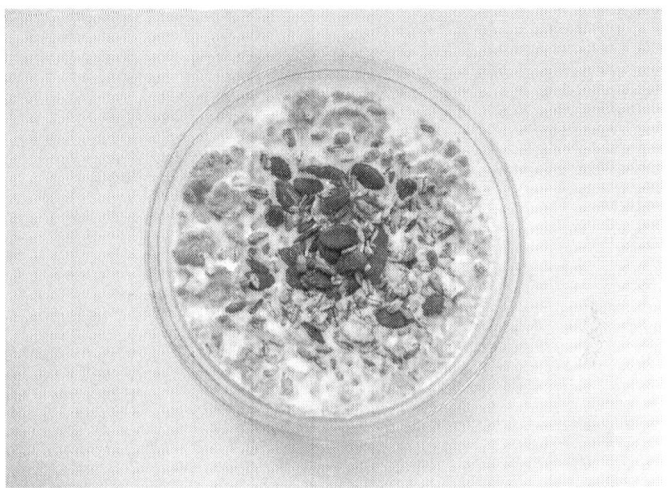

Ingredients

½ cup of coconut milk
1 tbsp hemp seeds
1 tbsp chia seeds
1 tbsp cranberries, dried
1 tbsp buckwheat

Directions

1. In a bowl, mix all the ingredients and enjoy.

Nutrition Facts

Servings: 1

Amount per serving

Calories 440

% Daily Value*

Total Fat 40.6g — 52%

Saturated Fat 26.2g — 131%

Cholesterol 0mg — 0%

Sodium 18mg — 1%

Total Carbohydrate 18.1g — 7%

Dietary Fiber 8.9g — 32%

Total Sugars 4.4g

Protein 11.4g

Vitamin D 0mcg — 0%

Calcium 150mg — 12%

Iron 5mg — 29%

Potassium 583mg — 12%

*The % Daily Value (DV) tells you how much a nutrient in a food serving contributes to a daily diet. 2,000 calorie a day is used for general nutrition advice.

10. Germ and Berries Parfait

Serves: 1

Ingredients

1 cup of coconut yogurt
2 tbsp wheat germ
50g raspberries
50g blackberries

Directions

1. Mix everything well and enjoy.

Nutrition Facts

Servings: 1

Amount per serving

Calories   211

	% Daily Value*
Total Fat 6g	8%
Saturated Fat 2.8g	14%
Cholesterol 0mg	0%
Sodium 2mg	0%
Total Carbohydrate 31.5g	11%
Dietary Fiber 8g	29%
Total Sugars 19g	
Protein 9.3g	
Vitamin D 0mcg	0%
Calcium 33mg	3%
Iron 2mg	11%
Potassium 290mg	6%

*The % Daily Value (DV) tells you how much a nutrient in a food serving contributes to a daily diet. 2,000 calorie a day is used for general nutrition advice.

11. Apple Pancakes

Serves: 4

Ingredients

2 tablespoons oil
1 1/2 cups soy milk
1 1/2 cups flour

1/2 cup tofu
1/3 cup vegetable shortening
2 1/2 teaspoons baking powder
1/2 teaspoon nutmeg
1/2 teaspoon salt
1/2 teaspoon cinnamon
2 apples, chopped
1/3 cup pecans, chopped

Directions

1. In a blender, blend together all ingredients except pecans until apples are minced.

2. Chop the apples by hand and mix together the ingredients. Gently mix in pecans.

3. Drop by spoonful's onto a lightly oiled griddle and cook for a few minutes, until bubbles appear.

4. Flip and cook until both sides are golden brown.

Nutrition Facts

Servings: 4

Amount per serving

Calories 523

% Daily Value*

Total Fat 28.8g	**37%**
Saturated Fat 6.7g	**34%**
Cholesterol 0mg	**0%**
Sodium 344mg	**15%**
Total Carbohydrate 59.4g	**22%**
Dietary Fiber 5.2g	**19%**
Total Sugars 15.7g	
Protein 9.7g	
Vitamin D 0mcg	0%
Calcium 203mg	16%
Iron 4mg	22%
Potassium 630mg	13%

*The % Daily Value (DV) tells you how much a nutrient in a food serving contributes to a daily diet. 2,000 calorie a day is used for general nutrition advice.

12. Berry Beet Smoothie Bowl

Serves: 2

Ingredients

½ cup almond milk
1 tbsp flax meal
¾ cup beets, roasted and chopped
¾ cup raspberries, frozen
Juice of 2 limes
1 scoop vanilla protein powder
1 banana
Toppings:
Banana, sliced
Coconut flakes
Slivered almonds

Directions

1. In a blender, blend all the ingredients and pour into a bowl.

2. Add the toppings and enjoy!

Nutrition Facts

Servings: 2

Amount per serving

Calories 407

% Daily Value*

Total Fat 18g	23%
Saturated Fat 13.9g	70%
Cholesterol 1mg	0%
Sodium 96mg	4%
Total Carbohydrate 52.1g	19%
Dietary Fiber 12.1g	43%
Total Sugars 26.1g	
Protein 19.4g	
Vitamin D 0mcg	0%
Calcium 131mg	10%
Iron 3mg	16%
Potassium 1015mg	22%

*The % Daily Value (DV) tells you how much a nutrient in a food serving contributes to a daily diet. 2,000 calorie a day is used for general nutrition advice.

13. Chocolate Chia Seeds Pudding

Serves: 1

Ingredients

2 tbsp chia seeds
⅓ cup almond milk
⅓ cup coconut milk
1 scoop chocolate protein powder
1 tbsp maple syrup
Cacao nibs and sliced bananas for topping

Directions

1. In a bowl, mix all the ingredients and cover.

2. Keep in the fridge for at least 15 minutes.

3. Top with cacao nibs and banana slices. Enjoy.

Nutrition Facts

Servings: 1

Amount per serving
Calories   565

% Daily Value*

Total Fat 46.9g	60%
Saturated Fat 33.3g	167%
Cholesterol 20mg	7%
Sodium 104mg	5%
Total Carbohydrate 34.1g	12%
Dietary Fiber 12.1g	43%
Total Sugars 15.6g	
Protein 19.5g	

Vitamin D 0mcg	0%
Calcium 348mg	27%
Iron 7mg	40%
Potassium 725mg	15%

*The % Daily Value (DV) tells you how much a nutrient in a food serving contributes to a daily diet. 2,000 calorie a day is used for general nutrition advice.

14. Gluten-Free Pancakes

Serves: 4

Ingredients

- 1 cup oat flour
- 2 tsp baking powder
- ¾ cup peanut butter
- 1 cup unsweetened almond milk
- 1 tbsp flaxseed meal
- 2 tsp agave
- 2 tbsp plain coconut yogurt

Directions

1. In a bowl, mix together flour, and baking powder.
2. Add the almond milk, agave, flaxseed meal, and yogurt. Stir until smooth.
3. Heat a nonstick skillet on medium heat.
4. Pour almost 1/4 cup of pancake batter at a time into the skillet. When bubbles begin to form on top of each pancake, flip it and cook an extra 1-2 minutes until it's cooked through.
5. Serve the pancakes and top with fresh fruit and additional agave.

Nutrition Facts

Servings: 4

Amount per serving

Calories 414

% Daily Value*

Total Fat 27.5g	**35%**
Saturated Fat 5.9g	**30%**
Cholesterol 0mg	**0%**
Sodium 276mg	**12%**
Total Carbohydrate 31.8g	**12%**
Dietary Fiber 6.2g	**22%**
Total Sugars 8.6g	
Protein 15.7g	
Vitamin D 0mcg	2%
Calcium 213mg	16%
Iron 7mg	36%
Potassium 707mg	15%

The % Daily Value (DV) tells you how much a nutrient in a food serving contributes to a daily diet. 2,000 calorie a day is used for general nutrition advice.

15. Carrot Cake Overnight Oats

Serves: 2

Ingredients

- 1 cup raw oats
- ⅓ cup vanilla whey protein powder
- ½ cup carrots, shredded
- 2 cup almond milk
- ½ cup of coconut yogurt
- 2 tbsp raisins
- 6 tbsp walnut, pieces
- 3 tbsp stevia
- 1 tsp Apple Pie Spice
- 1 tsp cinnamon

Directions

1. Mix all ingredients in a bowl and stir until combined.
2. Divide evenly and put in containers. Keep in the fridge for 5 hours.
3. Enjoy.

Desserts

1. Coffee Chia Pudding

Serves: 1

Ingredients

- 1 scoop chocolate protein powder
- 2 tbsp chia seeds
- 1 cup cold coffee, brewed
- 1 tbsp stevia

Directions

1. In a bowl, mix protein powder, coffee, chia seeds, and stevia. Stir well.

2. Keep in the fridge for 2 hours or until chia seeds thicken up. Enjoy!

Nutrition Facts

Servings: 1

Amount per serving

Calories   195

% Daily Value*

Total Fat 9.5g   12%

   Saturated Fat 1.4g   7%

Cholesterol 20mg   7%

Sodium 89mg   4%

Total Carbohydrate 13.9g   5%

   Dietary Fiber 10.1g   36%

   Total Sugars 1g

Protein 15g

Vitamin D 0mcg   0%

Calcium 251mg   19%

Iron 3mg   15%

Potassium 331mg   7%

*The % Daily Value (DV) tells you how much a nutrient in a food serving contributes to a daily diet. 2,000 calorie a day is used for general nutrition advice.

2. Protein Brownies

Serves: 18

Ingredients

20 oz. soy milk
24 grams of flax meal
90 grams of buckwheat flour
30 grams of tapioca flour
113 grams applesauce, unsweetened
1 tbsp vanilla extract
24 grams stevia
200 grams of chocolate protein powder
80 grams of cacao powder
1 tsp baking soda
1 tsp salt
90 grams of chocolate chips, vegan

Directions

1. Preheat your oven to 350 F and line a baking sheet.

2. In a bowl, mix all the dry ingredients and keep aside. In another bowl, mix all the wet ingredients.
3. Now, mix all the wet ingredients with the dry until well mixed.
4. Transfer all the batter in the baking pan and bake for 40 minutes.
5. Cool the brownies and, then cut into pieces. Serve and enjoy!

Nutrition Facts

Servings: 18

Amount per serving

Calories 121

% Daily Value*

Total Fat 3.3g	4%
Saturated Fat 1.5g	8%
Cholesterol 17mg	6%
Sodium 283mg	12%
Total Carbohydrate 12.8g	5%
Dietary Fiber 1.7g	6%
Total Sugars 5.5g	
Protein 10.3g	
Vitamin D 0mcg	0%
Calcium 75mg	6%
Iron 1mg	5%
Potassium 181mg	4%

The % Daily Value (DV) tells you how much a nutrient in a food serving contributes to a daily diet. 2,000 calorie a day is used for general nutrition advice.

3. Warm Blueberry Yogurt

Serves: 1

Ingredients

½ cup blueberries
¾ cup coconut yogurt
1 tsp stevia
40g protein powder

Directions

1. In a microwave, heat the blueberries for 1 minute.

2. Add protein powder, stevia, and coconut yogurt on blueberries and mix well. Serve.

Nutrition Facts

Servings: 1

Amount per serving

Calories   256

	% Daily Value*
Total Fat 6.9g	9%
Saturated Fat 3.9g	20%
Cholesterol 100mg	33%
Sodium 87mg	4%
Total Carbohydrate 17.8g	6%
Dietary Fiber 1.8g	6%
Total Sugars 9.9g	
Protein 32.6g	
Vitamin D 0mcg	0%
Calcium 180mg	14%
Iron 2mg	11%
Potassium 282mg	6%

*The % Daily Value (DV) tells you how much a nutrient in a food serving contributes to a daily diet. 2,000 calorie a day is used for general nutrition advice.

4. Pumpkin Spice Mug Cake

Serves: 1

Ingredients

2 tbsp stevia
45 grams of buckwheat flour
30 grams of wheat gluten
60 grams of pumpkin puree
½ tsp pumpkin spice
½ tsp baking soda
½ tsp baking powder
1 tsp apple cider vinegar
Pinch of salt
1 cup of water

Directions

1. In a microwave bowl, mix buckwheat flour, stevia, gelatin, pumpkin spice, baking powder, salt, and baking soda. Stir until well mixed.

2. Nox, add the water, vinegar, and pumpkin puree to the dry ingredients and mix well.
3. Bake in the oven for 2 minutes or until formed exactly like a cake.
4. Enjoy!

Nutrition Facts

Servings: 1

Amount per serving

Calories   298

	% Daily Value*
Total Fat 2.2g	3%
Saturated Fat 0.5g	2%
Cholesterol 0mg	0%
Sodium 811mg	35%
Total Carbohydrate 44.4g	16%
Dietary Fiber 6.4g	23%
Total Sugars 3.2g	
Protein 29.4g	
Vitamin D 0mcg	0%
Calcium 156mg	12%
Iron 3mg	17%
Potassium 647mg	14%

*The % Daily Value (DV) tells you how much a nutrient in a food serving contributes to a daily diet. 2,000 calorie a day is used for general nutrition advice.

5. Almond and Orange Creamsicle

Serves: 4

Ingredients

½ cup of orange juice, fresh squeezed
¼ cup natural almond butter
1 cup of coconut yogurt

Directions

1. Blend all ingredients in a blender until smooth.
2. Pour into popsicle molds and keep in the freezer for 7 hours or overnight.

Nutrition Facts

Servings: 4

Amount per serving

Calories   140

                               % Daily Value*

Total Fat 10.3g   13%

    Saturated Fat 1.5g   8%

Cholesterol 0mg   0%

Sodium 71mg   3%

Total Carbohydrate 10g   4%

    Dietary Fiber 0.6g   **2%**

    Total Sugars 6.7g

Protein 3.6g

Vitamin D 0mcg   0%

Calcium 43mg   3%

Iron 1mg   5%

Potassium 180mg   4%

The % Daily Value (DV) tells you how much a nutrient in a food serving contributes to a daily diet. <u>2,000 calorie a day</u> is used for general nutrition advice.

6. Date and Cashew Truffle

Serves: 4

Ingredients

8 Medjool dates, pitted
1 cup cashews, soaked
3 tbsp raw cacao powder
3 tbsp cacao nibs

Directions

1. Drain cashews, then mix in a processor with the dates. Blend until smooth.
2. Add the cacao nibs and process a few times to mix everything. Roll the mixture into balls and dust with cacao powder. Enjoy!

Nutrition Facts

Servings: 4

Amount per serving
Calories 664

	% Daily Value*
Total Fat 33.1g	**42%**
Saturated Fat 40.6g	**203%**
Cholesterol 0mg	**0%**
Sodium 33mg	**1%**
Total Carbohydrate 83.7g	**30%**
Dietary Fiber 29.5g	**105%**
Total Sugars 56.5g	
Protein 14g	
Vitamin D 0mcg	0%
Calcium 100mg	8%
Iron 6mg	31%
Potassium 903mg	19%

*The % Daily Value (DV) tells you how much a nutrient in a food serving contributes to a daily diet. 2,000 calorie a day is used for general nutrition advice.

7. Avocado Ice Cream

Serves: 4

Ingredients

- 1 small avocado
- ¼ cup of coconut milk
- ⅓ tbsp coconut yogurt
- ¼ cup peanut butter
- 2 tbsp agave
- 2 tsp lime juice

Directions

1. Mix all ingredients in a blender and blend until smooth.

2. Pour the mixture to a bowl and freeze for 4 hours.

3. Enjoy!

Nutrition Facts

Servings: 4

Amount per serving

Calories 265

% Daily Value*

Total Fat 21.7g — 28%

 Saturated Fat 7.1g — **36%**

Cholesterol 0mg — 0%

Sodium 80mg — 3%

Total Carbohydrate 16.9g — 6%

 Dietary Fiber 5.3g — **19%**

 Total Sugars 10.1g

Protein 5.3g

Vitamin D 0mcg — 0%

Calcium 18mg — 1%

Iron 2mg — 12%

Potassium 388mg — 8%

The % Daily Value (DV) tells you how much a nutrient in a food serving contributes to a daily diet. 2,000 calorie a day is used for general nutrition advice.

8. Mocha Pops

Serves: 4

Ingredients

1¼ cup coffee, brewed
1 cup coconut yogurt
⅓ cup dates, chopped
2 scoop vanilla whey protein powder
3 tbsp cocoa powder

1 tsp cinnamon
1 tsp vanilla extract

Directions

1. Add coffee and dates in a blender and let sit for almost 30 minutes. Add yogurt, cocoa powder, protein powder, vanilla, and cinnamon to blender container and blend until smooth.
2. Evenly divide the mixture into popsicle molds. Insert sticks and freeze for almost 8 hours.
3. Enjoy!

Nutrition Facts

Servings: 4

Amount per serving

Calories 142

	% Daily Value*
Total Fat 2.6g	3%
Saturated Fat 1.2g	6%
Cholesterol 28mg	9%
Sodium 42mg	2%
Total Carbohydrate 18.4g	7%
Dietary Fiber 2.7g	10%
Total Sugars 13.4g	
Protein 13.3g	
Vitamin D 0mcg	0%
Calcium 94mg	7%
Iron 1mg	5%
Potassium 363mg	8%

*The % Daily Value (DV) tells you how much a nutrient in a food serving contributes to a daily diet. 2,000 calorie a day is used for general nutrition advice.

9. Frozen Strawberry Yogurt

Serves: 2

Ingredients

⅓ cup of coconut yogurt
2 cup strawberries, frozen
2 tbsp agave syrup
2 tsp lemon juice

Directions

1. Process all ingredients in a food processor until smooth.
2. Serve in a bowl or store in your freezer.

Nutrition Facts

Servings: 2

Amount per serving

Calories 139

% Daily Value*

Total Fat 3.4g	4%
Saturated Fat 0g	0%
Cholesterol 0mg	0%
Sodium 17mg	1%
Total Carbohydrate 28.9g	11%
Dietary Fiber 3g	11%
Total Sugars 7.2g	
Protein 1.4g	
Vitamin D 0mcg	0%
Calcium 28mg	2%
Iron 1mg	4%
Potassium 239mg	5%

*The % Daily Value (DV) tells you how much a nutrient in a food serving contributes to a daily diet. 2,000 calorie a day is used for general nutrition advice.

10. Banana Maple Cookies

Serves: 2

Ingredients

½ cup, mashed banana
½ cup coconut flour
¼ cup maple syrup
¼ cup natural almond butter

Directions

1. Preheat your oven to 350 degrees F.
2. Mix the coconut flour and banana in a bowl.
3. In a small bowl, mix the syrup and almond butter and melt in the oven.
4. Mix the liquid ingredients into the coconut flour and banana mix.
5. Make small balls and place on a lined cookie sheet.
6. Press the balls flat and bake for 10 minutes or until golden.

Nutrition Facts

Servings: 8

Amount per serving

Calories 110

% Daily Value*

Total Fat 6.7g | 9%

Saturated Fat 0.9g | 4%

Cholesterol 0mg | 0%

Sodium 5mg | 0%

Total Carbohydrate 10.2g | 4%

Dietary Fiber 2.3g | 8%

Total Sugars 6.8g

Protein 3.1g

Vitamin D 4mcg | 20%

Calcium 38mg | 3%

Iron 1mg | 6%

Potassium 24mg | 1%

---

*The % Daily Value (DV) tells you how much a nutrient in a food serving contributes to a daily diet. 2,000 calorie a day is used for general nutrition advice.

11. Coffee Avocado Pudding

Serves: 4

Ingredients

1½ avocado
¼ cup of coconut milk
6 tbsp cocoa powder
1 tsp instant coffee
6 tbsp sugar-free maple syrup
1 tsp vanilla extract

Directions

1. Blend all ingredients in a food processor until smooth.

2. Divide into individual portions, top with coarse salt, cover, and refrigerate overnight.

3. Enjoy!

Nutrition Facts

Servings: 4

Amount per serving
Calories 698

% Daily Value*

Total Fat 58.6g	75%
Saturated Fat 15.1g	76%
Cholesterol 0mg	0%
Sodium 23mg	1%
Total Carbohydrate 49.3g	18%
Dietary Fiber 21.3g	76%
Total Sugars 20g	
Protein 7.1g	
Vitamin D 0mcg	0%
Calcium 65mg	5%
Iron 4mg	20%
Potassium 1646mg	35%

*The % Daily Value (DV) tells you how much a nutrient in a food serving contributes to a daily diet. 2,000 calorie a day is used for general nutrition advice.

12. Protein Fudge

Serves: 8

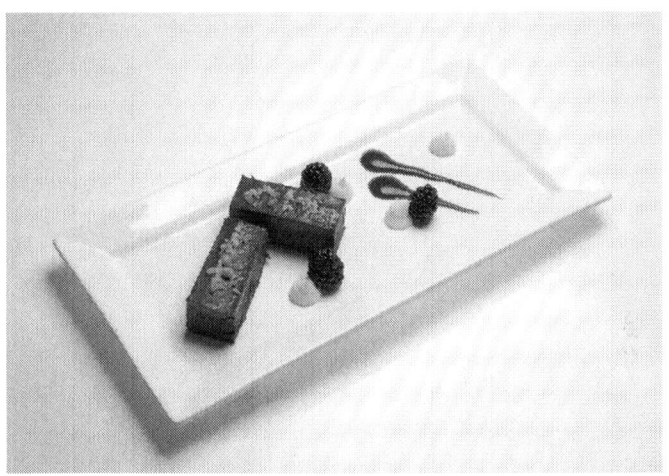

Ingredients

¼ cup almond milk
2 scoop Whey Chocolate Protein powder
½ cup chocolate-flavored hazelnut spread

Directions

1. Mix all the ingredients in a bowl.
2. Pour the mixture into a lined tray and freeze until set, almost an hour.
3. Cut into pieces and enjoy!

Nutrition Facts
Servings: 8

Amount per serving
Calories 121

	% Daily Value*
Total Fat 6.8g	9%
Saturated Fat 2.9g	15%
Cholesterol 1mg	0%
Sodium 27mg	1%
Total Carbohydrate 9.4g	3%
Dietary Fiber 0.6g	2%
Total Sugars 8.5g	
Protein 6.1g	
Vitamin D 0mcg	0%
Calcium 44mg	3%
Iron 0mg	3%
Potassium 20mg	0%

*The % Daily Value (DV) tells you how much a nutrient in a food serving contributes to a daily diet. 2,000 calorie a day is used for general nutrition advice.

13. Coconut Pumpkin Ice Cream

Serves: 4

Ingredients

½ cup vegan cheese
1½ cup pumpkin, canned
1 cup of coconut milk
½ cup of coconut yogurt
3 drop liquid Stevia
1 tsp cinnamon
¼ cup pecans, chopped
½ tsp pumpkin pie spice

Directions

1. Mix all ingredients in a blender and blend until smooth.

2. Pour mixture in a covered box in the freezer. Mix every half hour until desired consistency is attained.

Nutrition Facts

Servings: 4

Amount per serving
Calories 289

% Daily Value*

Total Fat 17.6g | 23%

   Saturated Fat 13.6g | **68%**

Cholesterol 0mg | 0%

Sodium 41mg | 2%

Total Carbohydrate 33.7g | 12%

   Dietary Fiber 11.9g | **42%**

   Total Sugars 14.9g

Protein 6g

Vitamin D 0mcg | 0%

Calcium 111mg | 9%

Iron 6mg | 32%

Potassium 863mg | 18%

The % Daily Value (DV) tells you how much a nutrient in a food serving contributes to a daily diet. 2,000 calorie a day is used for general nutrition advice.

14. Protein Crepes

Serves: 2

Ingredients

2 whole egg
½ scoop whey protein powder

Directions

1. Mix in a bowl two egg whites with half a scoop of protein powder. Stir well and pour onto a non-stick and cook. Flip with a spatula once the edges begin to bubble.

2. Remove from the pan and smear with almond butter, sliced apples and a sprinkling of cinnamon.

Nutrition Facts

Servings: 2

Amount per serving

Calories 93

% Daily Value*

Total Fat 4.8g — 6%

Saturated Fat 1.6g — 8%

Cholesterol 180mg — 60%

Sodium 75mg — 3%

Total Carbohydrate 1.3g — 0%

Dietary Fiber 0g — 0%

Total Sugars 0.6g

Protein 11.1g

Vitamin D 15mcg — 77%

Calcium 48mg — 4%

Iron 1mg — 6%

Potassium 103mg — 2%

The % Daily Value (DV) tells you how much a nutrient in a food serving contributes to a daily diet. 2,000 calorie a day is used for general nutrition advice.

15. Pumpkin Pie Soft Serve

Serves: 2

Ingredients

4 tbsp pumpkin puree
1¼ cup almond milk
1 scoop of protein powder
2 tbsp Walden Farms Syrup
1 to taste nutmeg
⅛ tsp pumpkin pie spice
2 tbsp bread crumbs

Directions

1. Add all ingredients in a blender. Blend until well mixed.
2. Pour mixture into ice cream maker.
3. Allow mixture to churn for 10 minutes.

Nutrition Facts

Servings: 2

Amount per serving

Calories   585

% Daily Value*

Total Fat 51.7g	**66%**
Saturated Fat 45.1g	**226%**
Cholesterol 32mg	**11%**
Sodium 166mg	**7%**
Total Carbohydrate 21.7g	**8%**
Dietary Fiber 6g	**22%**
Total Sugars 9.1g	
Protein 17.2g	
Vitamin D 0mcg	0%
Calcium 111mg	9%
Iron 5mg	26%
Potassium 724mg	15%

*The % Daily Value (DV) tells you how much a nutrient in a food serving contributes to a daily diet. 2,000 calorie a day is used for general nutrition advice.

Lunch Recipes

1. Wild Rice Salad

Serves: 4

Ingredients

    1 cup of wild rice
    ½ cup vegetable broth
    2 carrots
    1 cup pak choi
    1 cup broccoli
    1 cup young beans
    1 cup bean sprouts
    1 chili
    Juice of 1 fresh lime
    Some basil and sea salt to taste
    Cilantro

Directions

1. Chop all the vegetables and steam fry them in some vegetable broth in a pot until they are little bit cooked but still crunchy.

2. In the meantime, mortar the cilantro and the finely chopped chili.

3. Add lime juice until you have a smooth dressing.

4. Place the rice on a plate, add the greens and sprinkle the dressing on top.

5. It's that simple! Serve warm and enjoy!

Nutrition Facts

Servings: 4

Amount per serving

Calories 201

% Daily Value*

Total Fat 1.1g	**1%**
Saturated Fat 0.2g	**1%**
Cholesterol 0mg	**0%**
Sodium 146mg	**6%**
Total Carbohydrate 40.9g	**15%**
Dietary Fiber 5.3g	**19%**
Total Sugars 4.4g	
Protein 10.5g	
Vitamin D 0mcg	0%
Calcium 75mg	6%
Iron 2mg	12%
Potassium 633mg	13%

*The % Daily Value (DV) tells you how much a nutrient in a food serving contributes to a daily diet. 2,000 calorie a day is used for general nutrition advice.

2. Red Lentil Soup

Serves: 4

Ingredients

- 1 tbsp olive oil
- 1 cup red lentils, rinsed
- 2 cups of water
- 4 cups vegetable broth
- 3 carrots, diced
- 1 onion, diced
- 3 celery sticks, diced
- 1 tbsp tomato paste
- Sea salt to taste
- 1 tsp cumin
- 1 tsp chili powder
- 1 bay leaf
- 2 tbsp lemon juice

Directions

1. In an instant pot, sauté the onion, celery, carrots, and salt. Fry for 5 minutes.
2. Add chili powder, cumin, and tomato paste. Stir well.
3. Add lentils, broth, bay leaves, and water. Mix and close the lid. Cook for 10 minutes over high heat.
4. Release the pressure and open the lid.
5. Mx in lemon juice and serve.

Nutrition Facts

Servings: 4

Amount per serving

Calories 282

% Daily Value*

Total Fat 5.8g 7%

  Saturated Fat 1.1g 5%

Cholesterol 0mg 0%

Sodium 898mg 39%

Total Carbohydrate 39.3g 14%

  Dietary Fiber 17.3g 62%

  Total Sugars 6.2g

Protein 18.5g

Vitamin D 0mcg 0%

Calcium 83mg 6%

Iron 5mg 28%

Potassium 1003mg 21%

The % Daily Value (DV) tells you how much a nutrient in a food serving contributes to a daily diet. 2,000 calorie a day is used for general nutrition advice.

3. Tomato Spelt Pasta

Serves: 2

Ingredients

3 tbsp olive oil
⅔ cup vegetable broth
300g spelt pasta
1 eggplant, diced
1 zucchini, diced
2 garlic cloves, crushed
1 onion, diced
3 tomatoes, diced
⅔ cup sundried tomatoes
1 tsp oregano
2 tsp basil leaves, dried
Sea salt and pepper to taste

Directions

1. In a pan, heat the oil over medium heat. Fry garlic, onion, and eggplant for 10 minutes.

2. Add zucchini, tomatoes, sun dried tomatoes, and oregano. Cook for 8 minutes while stirring.

3. Cook the pasta until soft.

4. In a pan, add the broth and season with basil leaves, salt, and pepper. Let simmer for a few minutes.

5. Serve pasta with pasta sauce and enjoy!

Nutrition Facts

Servings: 2

Amount per serving
Calories 934

% Daily Value*

Total Fat 24.7g	32%
Saturated Fat 3.3g	17%
Cholesterol 0mg	0%
Sodium 658mg	29%
Total Carbohydrate 153.4g	56%
Dietary Fiber 20.5g	73%
Total Sugars 22.8g	
Protein 34.2g	
Vitamin D 0mcg	0%
Calcium 108mg	8%
Iron 4mg	21%
Potassium 2012mg	43%

*The % Daily Value (DV) tells you how much a nutrient in a food serving contributes to a daily diet. 2,000 calorie a day is used for general nutrition advice.

4. Chickpea Falafel

Serves: 6

Ingredients

1 tbsp olive oil
800g chickpeas, drained
4 tbsp buckwheat flour
4 spring onions, diced
A handful of parsley leaves
A handful of dill leaves
2 tsp of baking soda
1 tsp paprika
2 tsp cumin
1 tsp cayenne pepper
Sea salt and pepper to taste

Directions

1. Preheat the oven to 180 C and line a baking sheet with parchment paper.

2. In a blender, blend all the ingredients until very smooth.
3. Make small balls from this mixture and brush each ball with olive oil.
4. Bake in the oven for 20 minutes or until golden.
5. Serve on salads, sandwiches, or pita bread.

Nutrition Facts

Servings: 6

Amount per serving
Calories   530

% Daily Value*

Total Fat 10.8g	**14%**
Saturated Fat 1.2g	**6%**
Cholesterol 0mg	**0%**
Sodium 455mg	**20%**
Total Carbohydrate 85.9g	**31%**
Dietary Fiber 24.3g	**87%**
Total Sugars 14.7g	
Protein 26.8g	
Vitamin D 0mcg	0%
Calcium 158mg	12%
Iron 9mg	51%
Potassium 1254mg	27%

*The % Daily Value (DV) tells you how much a nutrient in a food serving contributes to a daily diet. 2,000 calorie a day is used for general nutrition advice.

5. Alkaline Gravy

Serves: 4

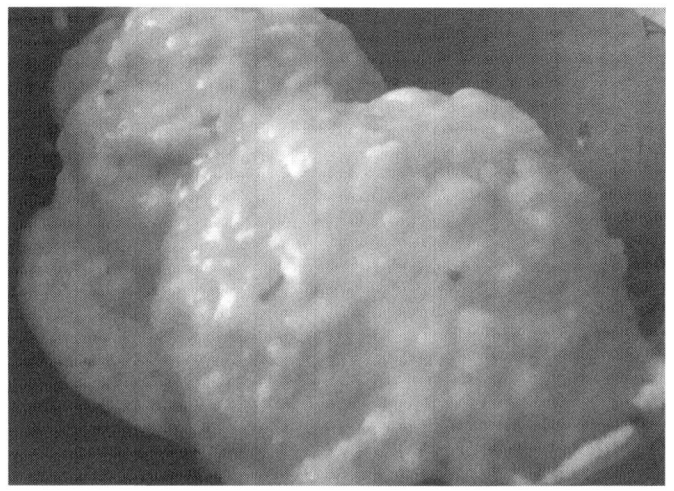

Ingredients

- 1 cup of white beans, drained
- 1 cup of vegetable broth
- 1 cup of soy milk
- 3 tbsp liquid aminos
- 1 tsp dried garlic
- 2 tsp dried onion
- 2 tbsp coconut flour
- 1 tbsp mixed herbs

Directions

1. In a good quality blender, blend beans, milk, broth, liquid aminos, garlic, onion, salt, and pepper until smooth.

2. In a large pan, over medium heat, add the gravy and cook. Add flour, herbs, and salt. Keep stirring during this process. Cook for 5 minutes.
3. Serve hot with alkaline biscuits.

Nutrition Facts

Servings: 4

Amount per serving

Calories 236

	% Daily Value*
Total Fat 2g	3%
Saturated Fat 0.4g	2%
Cholesterol 0mg	0%
Sodium 232mg	10%
Total Carbohydrate 39.2g	14%
Dietary Fiber 9g	32%
Total Sugars 3.8g	
Protein 16.7g	
Vitamin D 0mcg	0%
Calcium 149mg	11%
Iron 7mg	37%
Potassium 1110mg	24%

*The % Daily Value (DV) tells you how much a nutrient in a food serving contributes to a daily diet. 2,000 calorie a day is used for general nutrition advice.

6. Quinoa with Acorn Squash

Serves: 4

Ingredients

3/4 cup of quinoa, cooked
3/4 cup pomegranate seeds
1/4 cup raisins
1 acorn or kabocha squash
2 teaspoons minced fresh parsley
2 scallions, green parts only, chopped
1/4 cup olive oil, plus more for roasting squash
Zest of half a lemon
2 tablespoons lemon juice
Salt and pepper

Directions

1. Preheat your oven to 400 degrees. Line a baking sheet with foil.

2. Cut the top and bottom off the squash. Cut the acorn squash in half lengthwise and, with a spoon, scoop out the seeds. Cut each piece in half lengthwise.

3. Cut each quarter lengthwise, creating 1/2-inch slices. Put squash slices into a bowl and drizzle with olive oil and a sprinkle of salt.

4. Spread across the pan and arrange so each piece sits flat. Cook in the oven for 20 minutes.

5. In the meantime, make the dressing by whisking together the 1/4 cup of olive oil, parsley, lemon juice, lemon zest, and scallions. Season with salt and pepper, to taste.

6. Once the acorn squash is done, remove from the oven and cool for a few minutes.

7. Stir together the cooked quinoa, raisins, pomegranate seeds, and dressing in a bowl. Season with salt and pepper, to taste.

8. Top with roasted squash pieces and enjoy!

Nutrition Facts

Servings: 4

Amount per serving

Calories   264

	% Daily Value*
Total Fat 14.7g	19%
Saturated Fat 2.1g	11%
Cholesterol 0mg	0%
Sodium 6mg	0%
Total Carbohydrate 29.8g	11%
Dietary Fiber 3.1g	11%
Total Sugars 6.8g	
Protein 5.4g	
Vitamin D 0mcg	0%
Calcium 31mg	2%
Iron 2mg	10%
Potassium 358mg	8%

*The % Daily Value (DV) tells you how much a nutrient in a food serving contributes to a daily diet. 2,000 calorie a day is used for general nutrition advice.

7. Tempeh Lettuce Wraps

Serves: 4

Ingredients

1 tablespoon peanut oil
1 (8-ounce) package tempeh, crumbled
1 tablespoon lime juice
2 tablespoons hoisin sauce
3/4 cup diced mango
1/2 cup cucumber, seeded and diced
1/4 cup cashews, chopped and roasted
8 lettuce leaves
1/4 cup mint leaves, chopped

Directions

1. Heat the oil in over medium-high heat.

2. Add the tempeh and cook, stirring, until lightly browned, about 2 minutes. Stir in the hoisin sauce and lime juice; remove from heat.

3. Divide the tempeh, mango, cucumber, cashews and mint leaves into 8 lettuce leaves. Drizzle with sweet chili sauce and serve.

Nutrition Facts

Servings: 4

Amount per serving

Calories 232

% Daily Value*

Total Fat 13.9g	**18%**
Saturated Fat 2.7g	**14%**
Cholesterol 0mg	**0%**
Sodium 139mg	**6%**
Total Carbohydrate 17.7g	**6%**
Dietary Fiber 1.5g	**5%**
Total Sugars 7.2g	
Protein 12.7g	
Vitamin D 0mcg	0%
Calcium 86mg	7%
Iron 3mg	18%
Potassium 403mg	9%

The % Daily Value (DV) tells you how much a nutrient in a food serving contributes to a daily diet. 2,000 calorie a day is used for general nutrition advice.

8. Broccoli Salad

Serves: 6

Ingredients

2 heads broccoli, cut into florets
½ cup green onions, chopped
2 cups cabbage, chopped
½ cup raisins

Dressing:

2 tbsp miso
2 tbsp coconut butter
1 shallot
2 tablespoons canola oil

Directions

1. Mix all the salad ingredients in a bowl.

2. Process the dressing ingredients in a food processor until smooth. Pour over the salad ingredients and mix well to combine.
3. Serve!

Nutrition Facts

Servings: 6

Amount per serving

Calories   **173**

	% Daily Value*
Total Fat 11.1g	14%
Saturated Fat 5.8g	29%
Cholesterol 0mg	0%
Sodium 230mg	10%
Total Carbohydrate 18.1g	7%
Dietary Fiber 4g	14%
Total Sugars 10g	
Protein 2.7g	
Vitamin D 0mcg	0%
Calcium 36mg	3%
Iron 1mg	6%
Potassium 165mg	4%

The % Daily Value (DV) tells you how much a nutrient in a food serving contributes to a daily diet. 2,000 calorie a day is used for general nutrition advice.

9. Quinoa Bites

Serves: 6

Ingredients

Cooking spray
1 1/2 cups cooked quinoa
1/2 cup black beans
1/2 cup sweet potato puree
2 tbsp flaxseed powder
1 tablespoon cilantro, chopped
1 teaspoon paprika
1 teaspoon cumin
1/2 teaspoon garlic powder
1/8 teaspoon black pepper
1/2 teaspoon salt

Directions

1. Preheat your oven to 350 degrees F. Add all ingredients to a bowl and mix until everything is mixed.

2. Spray a muffin tin with cooking oil.

3. Spoon the mixture into the tins using a tablespoon, and pat down the top of each one.

4. Bake until cooked through and holding together, about 15mins. Enjoy!

Nutrition Facts

Servings: 6

Amount per serving

Calories 247

% Daily Value*

Total Fat 3.2g — 4%

   Saturated Fat 0.4g — 2%

Cholesterol 0mg — 0%

Sodium 214mg — 9%

Total Carbohydrate 44.2g — 16%

   Dietary Fiber 7.3g — 26%

   Total Sugars 1.6g

Protein 10.7g

Vitamin D 0mcg — 0%

Calcium 51mg — 4%

Iron 3mg — 19%

Potassium 542mg — 12%

*The % Daily Value (DV) tells you how much a nutrient in a food serving contributes to a daily diet. 2,000 calorie a day is used for general nutrition advice.

10. Lentil Jamaican Curry

Serves: 4

Ingredients

1 tsp oil
1 cup coconut milk
1/2 cup red lentils
15 oz can cannellini beans, cooked beans
1 onion, sliced or chopped
5 cloves garlic, chopped
A big handful of spinach
1/2 hot green chile, chopped
2 tsp Jamaican Curry powder
1/2 tsp turmeric
1 1/4 cup water
3/4 tsp salt
cayenne to taste

Directions

1. Heat oil in a skillet over medium heat.
2. Add the garlic, onion, chile. Cook until golden.
3. Add all the spices and cook for a few seconds.
4. Add the coconut milk, lentils, water, and salt. Bring to a boil.
5. Add the beans, and cook for 10 minutes until the lentils are cooked through. Add some water if needed.
6. Taste and adjust salt and spices.
7. Mix in the greens. Simmer for 2 minutes.
8. Add a dash of cayenne and lemon juice. Serve hot over rice.

Nutrition Facts

Servings: 4

Amount per serving

Calories 282

% Daily Value*

Total Fat 15.9g	20%
Saturated Fat 12.9g	65%
Cholesterol 0mg	0%
Sodium 503mg	22%
Total Carbohydrate 27.3g	10%
Dietary Fiber 12g	43%
Total Sugars 4.4g	
Protein 10.5g	
Vitamin D 0mcg	0%
Calcium 96mg	7%
Iron 4mg	25%
Potassium 740mg	16%

*The % Daily Value (DV) tells you how much a nutrient in a food serving contributes to a daily diet. 2,000 calorie a day is used for general nutrition advice.

11. African Lentil Stew

Serves: 4

Ingredients

- 1 tsp oil
- 1/2 cup red lentils
- 2.5 cups vegetable stock
- 2 cups mixed veggies, chopped
- 1/2 onion
- 2 juicy tomatoes
- 4 garlic cloves
- 1-inch ginger
- 1 tbsp Asian chili sauce
- 1 tbsp tomato paste or ketchup
- 1.5 tsp ground cumin
- 2 tsp ground coriander
- 1 tsp Harissa Spice Blend
- 1/4 tsp black pepper

2 tbsp peanuts
1/4 cup peanut butter
3/4 tsp to 1 salt
1 tsp lemon juice
1/2 cup packed baby spinach

Directions

1. Heat oil in a pan over medium heat.

2. Add onions and cook until soft 5 minutes.

3. Meanwhile, blend the tomatoes, ginger, garlic, chili sauce, tomato paste, spices until pureed.

4. Add to the saucepan. Cook for 5 to 6 minutes.

5. Add peanut butter, lentils, half of the nuts, veggies, stock, salt, and lemon juice. Mix and cook.

6. Cook for 15 minutes. Taste and adjust salt, heat and check if the veggies are done.

7. Mix in the baby spinach. Cook for 5 minutes or until the lentils is cooked through. Add more water if needed.

8. Garnish with the peanuts, cilantro, more lemon juice. Serve with flatbread.

Nutrition Facts

Servings: 4

Amount per serving

Calories 301

% Daily Value*

Total Fat 13.6g	17%
Saturated Fat 3.6g	18%
Cholesterol 0mg	0%
Sodium 2006mg	87%
Total Carbohydrate 35.2g	13%
Dietary Fiber 12.8g	46%
Total Sugars 9.7g	
Protein 15g	
Vitamin D 0mcg	0%
Calcium 76mg	6%
Iron 6mg	33%
Potassium 846mg	18%

*The % Daily Value (DV) tells you how much a nutrient in a food serving contributes to a daily diet. 2,000 calorie a day is used for general nutrition advice.

12. Mexican Burgers

Serves: 4

Ingredients

For the burger:

    4 whole grain burger buns, cut in half and toasted

4 lettuce, washed
2 medium tomatoes, sliced

For the patty:

2 tbsps. sunflower oil
10 ½ oz tempeh, mashed
½ cup sweet corn
1 cup cooked kidney beans, mashed
1 tsp chia seeds
2 tsp dried smoked paprika
4 tbsps. fresh parsley, thinly sliced
1 medium red bell pepper, diced
4 medium scallions, sliced
1 tbsp water

For the sauce:

6 tbsp vegan mayonnaise
1 ½ tsp Cajun spice

Directions

1. In a bowl, mix the chia seeds with the water and keep aside while you prepare the other ingredients.

2. In another bowl, mix all the ingredients for the patties except the oil.

3. Make the burger patties and grill them in oil for 3 minutes each side.

4. In a small bowl and mix the ingredients for the sauce.

5. For serving add sauce, sliced tomatoes, lettuce, and patty to the bun, enjoy!

Nutrition Facts

Servings: 4

Amount per serving

Calories 633

% Daily Value*

Total Fat 19.9g | 25%
Saturated Fat 2.9g | 15%
Cholesterol 0mg | 0%
Sodium 366mg | 16%
Total Carbohydrate 85.8g | 31%
Dietary Fiber 15.1g | 54%
Total Sugars 9.4g
Protein 34.4g

Vitamin D 0mcg | 0%
Calcium 342mg | 26%
Iron 9mg | 52%
Potassium 1323mg | 28%

The % Daily Value (DV) tells you how much a nutrient in a food serving contributes to a daily diet. 2,000 calorie a day is used for general nutrition advice.

13. Quinoa Salad with Mango

Serves: 3

Ingredients

½ cup kidney beans, cooked
½ cup quinoa
½ cup sweet corn
3 tbsps. goji berries, dried
1 mango, diced
1 red bell pepper, sliced
3½ oz salad greens
1¾ oz seed sprouts
1 oz walnut halves, crushed
1 cup of water

Directions

1. Boil the quinoa in 1 cup water until soft for 20 minutes.

2. Mix the quinoa with the kidney beans, goji berries, sweet corn, walnut halves, and the salad dressing.

3. Place the salad greens, bean sprouts, and bell pepper in a bowl and add the rest of the ingredients.

Nutrition Facts

Servings: 3

Amount per serving
Calories 498

	% Daily Value*
Total Fat 8.5g	**11%**
Saturated Fat 0.7g	**4%**
Cholesterol 0mg	**0%**
Sodium 62mg	**3%**
Total Carbohydrate 94.5g	**34%**
Dietary Fiber 17.7g	**63%**
Total Sugars 30.9g	
Protein 22.8g	
Vitamin D 0mcg	0%
Calcium 196mg	15%
Iron 8mg	45%
Potassium 958mg	20%

*The % Daily Value (DV) tells you how much a nutrient in a food serving contributes to a daily diet. 2,000 calorie a day is used for general nutrition advice.

14. Creamy Red Curry

Serves: 6

Ingredients

1 tablespoon coconut oil

1 can coconut milk
2 cups red lentils
2 cups veggie broth
1 cup onion, chopped
1/2 can diced tomatoes
1 tablespoon garlic, minced
2 medium carrots, chopped
5 tablespoons red curry paste

Directions

1. Set your instant pot to "Sauté." Add oil, garlic, onion, and carrots.

2. Cook for about 5 minutes until the onions are brown and the edges of the carrots are seared.

3. Add the red curry paste and the lentils, and stir everything together for 2 minutes.

4. Add the remaining ingredients and mix. Place on the top and set your instant pot on the "Pressure Cook" setting. Cook for 10 minutes for creamy lentils.

5. Season to taste with a bit of salt and pepper.

Nutrition Facts

Servings: 6

Amount per serving

Calories 511

% Daily Value*

Total Fat 25.8g	**33%**
Saturated Fat 20.2g	**101%**
Cholesterol 0mg	**0%**
Sodium 914mg	**40%**
Total Carbohydrate 53g	**19%**
Dietary Fiber 22.6g	**81%**
Total Sugars 7.5g	
Protein 18.8g	
Vitamin D 0mcg	0%
Calcium 76mg	6%
Iron 7mg	40%
Potassium 920mg	20%

*The % Daily Value (DV) tells you how much a nutrient in a food serving contributes to a daily diet. 2,000 calorie a day is used for general nutrition advice.

15. Sweet Potato Tots

Serves: 2

Ingredients

Olive oil spray
4 sweet potatoes
Sea salt to taste

Directions

1. Preheat the oven to 430F.

2. Peel the sweet potatoes.

3. In a pot, add water and bring it to boil. Add in the peeled sweet potatoes and boil them for 15 minutes.

4. Let the sweet potatoes cool at room temperature and grate the sweet potatoes into a bowl.

5. Grab a handful of the grated sweet potato and make a small tater tot. Repeat for the remaining grated sweet potato.

6. Arrange the tots on a baking rack, or nonstick baking sheet, then spray them with olive oil and sprinkle a little sea salt on top.

7. Bake for 40 minutes and flip them halfway through cooking to make sure all sides are crispy.

Nutrition Facts

Servings: 2

Amount per serving

Calories 67

% Daily Value*

Total Fat 0.3g	0%
Saturated Fat 0g	0%
Cholesterol 0mg	0%
Sodium 23mg	1%
Total Carbohydrate 16.5g	6%
Dietary Fiber 2g	7%
Total Sugars 3.5g	
Protein 1g	

Vitamin D 0mcg	0%
Calcium 10mg	1%
Iron 0mg	1%
Potassium 0mg	0%

*The % Daily Value (DV) tells you how much a nutrient in a food serving contributes to a daily diet. 2,000 calorie a day is used for general nutrition

16. Tabbouleh Salad

Serves: 4

Ingredients

- 1 1/4 cups bulgur wheat
- 2 cups shelled edamame
- 1 15-ounce can chickpeas, drained
- 2 cups water, boiling
- 1/4 cup prepared pesto
- 3 tbsp. fresh lemon juice
- 2 cups cherry tomatoes, chopped
- 1/3 cup green onions, sliced
- 2 tbsp. fresh parsley, minced
- 1/4 tsp. freshly ground black pepper

Directions

1. Mix the bulgur wheat and boiling water in a bowl. Cover and let stand 30 minutes. Drain.

2. Mix pesto and lemon juice; stir with a whisk. Mix bulgur, parsley, pesto mixture, tomatoes, chickpeas, green onions, peppers and edamame in a GBI bowl; and stir gently to combine.

3. Serve with pita.

Nutrition Facts

Servings: 4

Amount per serving
Calories 657

% Daily Value*

Total Fat 11.9g | 15%
 Saturated Fat 1.4g | 7%
Cholesterol 0mg | 0%
Sodium 68mg | 3%
Total Carbohydrate 109g | 40%
 Dietary Fiber 30.2g | 108%
 Total Sugars 15.9g
Protein 34.5g

Vitamin D 0mcg | 0%
Calcium 224mg | 17%
Iron 10mg | 53%
Potassium 1717mg | 37%

*The % Daily Value (DV) tells you how much a nutrient in a food serving contributes to a daily diet. 2,000 calorie a day is used for general nutrition advice.

17. White Bean Salad

Serves: 4

Ingredients

2 tablespoons olive oil
2 cans white beans, drained
1 red onion, minced
3 cloves garlic, minced
1/2 cup fresh parsley, chopped
2 tomatoes, diced
2 tablespoons vinegar
1/3 cup sliced black olives
1/2 lemon, juiced
Salt and black pepper to taste

Directions

1. Over low heat, mix the beans, onions, garlic, and parsley in olive oil. Heat for just 1 minute, or until fragrant.
2. Remove from heat and put in a large bowl.
3. Add the tomatoes, vinegar, black olives, and lemon juice and mix well and coat all ingredients.
4. Serve white bean salad warm or chilled.

Nutrition Facts

Servings: 4

Amount per serving

Calories 225

% Daily Value*

Total Fat 8.4g	**11%**
Saturated Fat 1.2g	6%
Cholesterol 0mg	**0%**
Sodium 207mg	**9%**
Total Carbohydrate 28.6g	**10%**
Dietary Fiber 12.2g	**44%**
Total Sugars 4.1g	
Protein 9.4g	
Vitamin D 0mcg	0%
Calcium 139mg	11%
Iron 3mg	17%
Potassium 253mg	5%

*The % Daily Value (DV) tells you how much a nutrient in a food serving contributes to a daily diet. 2,000 calorie a day is used for general nutrition advice.

Dinner Recipes

1. White Bean Gravy

Serves: 4

Ingredients

- 1 cup of white beans, drained
- 1 cup of vegetable broth
- 1 cup of soy milk
- 3 tbsp liquid aminos
- 1 tbsp nutritional yeast
- 1 tsp dried garlic
- 2 tsp dried onion
- 2 tbsp all-purpose flour
- 1 tbsp mixed herbs

Directions

1. In a good quality blender, blend beans, milk, broth, liquid aminos, yeast, garlic, onion, salt, and pepper until smooth.
2. In a large pan, over medium heat, add the gravy and cook. Add flour, herbs, and salt. Keep stirring during this process. Cook for 5 minutes.
3. Serve hot with biscuits.

Nutrition Facts

Servings: 4

Amount per serving

Calories 236

% Daily Value*

Total Fat 2g	3%
Saturated Fat 0.4g	2%
Cholesterol 0mg	0%
Sodium 232mg	10%
Total Carbohydrate 39.2g	14%
Dietary Fiber 9g	32%
Total Sugars 3.8g	
Protein 16.7g	
Vitamin D 0mcg	0%
Calcium 149mg	11%
Iron 7mg	37%
Potassium 1110mg	24%

*The % Daily Value (DV) tells you how much a nutrient in a food serving contributes to a daily diet. 2,000 calorie a day is used for general nutrition advice.

2. Vegetable Biryani

Serves: 3

Ingredients

2 tbsp. olive oil
2 cups of water
1 cup brown rice
½ cup frozen peas, thawed
½ onion, chopped
¼ tsp. turmeric
4 whole peppercorns
½ tsp. cumin seeds
1 tsp coriander
¼ Tsp. ginger powder
Salt to taste

Directions

1. In a skillet, heat the olive oil over medium heat and add onions. Fry for 2 minutes and then add the

peppercorns, cumin seeds, ginger, and coriander powder. Fry for 2 minutes until fragrant.
2. Add the rice with 2 cups of water and bring to a boil. Then reduce the heat, add the peas and simmer over low heat for almost 20 minutes or until rice is cooked and water is absorbed.
3. Stir well and serve with your favorite vegan sauce. Biryani tastes well with mint coriander chutney.

Nutrition Facts

Servings: 3

Amount per serving

Calories 340

% Daily Value*

Total Fat 11.2g	**14%**
Saturated Fat 1.7g	**9%**
Cholesterol 0mg	**0%**
Sodium 28mg	**1%**
Total Carbohydrate 54.1g	**20%**
Dietary Fiber 4.1g	**15%**
Total Sugars 2.1g	
Protein 6.4g	
Vitamin D 0mcg	0%
Calcium 40mg	3%
Iron 2mg	11%
Potassium 241mg	5%

The % Daily Value (DV) tells you how much a nutrient in a food serving contributes to a daily diet. 2,000 calorie a day is used for general nutrition advice.

3. Cauliflower Rice with Peas

Serves: 2

Ingredients

½ cup peas
1 small head cauliflower
2 scallions, sliced
¼ cup lemon juice
Zest of one lime
1 teaspoon cumin
1 teaspoon maple syrup
½-teaspoon fresh ginger (grated)
¼ cup pine nuts
½ tablespoon chili flakes
Salt and pepper to taste

Directions

1. Cut the cauliflower florets and process in a food processor until the cauliflower is the size of rice. Mix in peas and scallions.
2. In another bowl, mix lemon zest, lemon juice, maple syrup, cumin, and ginger. Pour this mixture over cauliflower mixture and stir well.
3. Sprinkle with pine nuts, salt, pepper, and chili flakes. Serve and enjoy!

Nutrition Facts

Servings: 2

Amount per serving
Calories 221

% Daily Value*

Total Fat 12.8g	16%
Saturated Fat 1.2g	6%
Cholesterol 0mg	0%
Sodium 50mg	2%
Total Carbohydrate 22.2g	8%
Dietary Fiber 8.4g	30%
Total Sugars 10.6g	
Protein 9.8g	
Vitamin D 0mcg	0%
Calcium 91mg	7%
Iron 4mg	21%
Potassium 791mg	17%

*The % Daily Value (DV) tells you how much a nutrient in a food serving contributes to a daily diet. 2,000 calorie a day is used for general nutrition advice.

4. Curried Vegetables

Serves: 4

Ingredients

2 teaspoons olive oil
1 can reduced fat coconut milk
1 -2 tablespoon fresh lime juice
1-cup low sodium vegetable broth
1 large onion, chopped
3 tablespoons tomato paste
1/2 cup frozen green pea
3 medium red potatoes scrubbed and cut into 1-inch chunks
1 package frozen cut green beans or fresh green beans
1 small cauliflower, cut into small florets
3 tablespoons mild curry powder

1/4 cup fresh cilantro, chopped
Cayenne pepper, to taste

Directions

1. Heat the oil in a pan over medium heat.
2. Add onion, and cook for 5 minutes, or until lightly browned, mixing frequently.
3. Add coconut milk and broth. Mix in tomato paste and curry powder. Bring to a boil.
4. Add potatoes, lower the heat to medium, cover and cook for 12 minutes, or until potatoes are a little bit firm.
5. Mix in green beans and cauliflower. Cover and cook 5 minutes more, or until vegetables are tender. Remove from the heat.
6. Mix in peas, cilantro, and lime juice. Add salt, pepper, and cayenne.
7. Serve with rice.

Nutrition Facts

Servings: 4

Amount per serving
Calories 273

	% Daily Value*
Total Fat 10.4g	13%
Saturated Fat 6.7g	34%
Cholesterol 0mg	0%
Sodium 142mg	6%
Total Carbohydrate 40.2g	15%
Dietary Fiber 8.9g	32%
Total Sugars 8.3g	
Protein 6.8g	
Vitamin D 0mcg	0%
Calcium 88mg	7%
Iron 4mg	20%
Potassium 1081mg	23%

The % Daily Value (DV) tells you how much a nutrient in a food serving contributes to a daily diet. 2,000 calorie a day is used for general nutrition advice.

5. Teriyaki Tofu Burger

Serves: 2

Ingredients

- 2 flatbread flat Out sandwich wraps
- 6 oz tofu, firm
- 1 tbsp sriracha
- 1 tbsp teriyaki, sauce, reduced sodium
- 1 tsp crushed red pepper flakes
- ¼ cup strips or slices carrots, sliced
- ¼ red onion, sliced
- 2 leaf, large lettuce

Directions

1. Heat your grill.

2. Marinate tofu in red chili flakes, teriyaki marinade, and Sriracha.

3. Fry red onion in a pan until soft.

4. Grill tofu for 3 min on each side.

5. Place on the wrap. Top with butter leaf lettuce, shredded carrots, and caramelized red onion.

Nutrition Facts

Servings: 2

Amount per serving

Calories 183

% Daily Value*

Total Fat 6.2g	8%
Saturated Fat 0.8g	4%
Cholesterol 0mg	0%
Sodium 785mg	34%
Total Carbohydrate 24g	9%
Dietary Fiber 10.7g	38%
Total Sugars 4g	
Protein 16.4g	
Vitamin D 0mcg	0%
Calcium 221mg	17%
Iron 3mg	19%
Potassium 222mg	5%

*The % Daily Value (DV) tells you how much a nutrient in a food serving contributes to a daily diet. 2,000 calorie a day is used for general nutrition advice.

6. Coconut Cashew Rice

Serves: 6

Ingredients

2 cup water
½ cup of brown rice
¼ cup cashews, crushed
2 cup light coconut milk
½ tsp salt
3 tbsp dried unsweetened coconut flakes

Directions

1. In a large pot, mix the rice, water, coconut milk, salt, and 2 tablespoons of coconut flakes.

2. Bring to a boil, then turn down the heat to low, cover, and let simmer for about 1 hour.

3. When the rice is cooked, fluff it with a fork, then mix in the cashews and the remaining coconut flakes.
4. Serve immediately.

Nutrition Facts

Servings: 6

Amount per serving

Calories 308

% Daily Value*

Total Fat 24.2g	31%
Saturated Fat 19.5g	97%
Cholesterol 0mg	0%
Sodium 231mg	10%
Total Carbohydrate 22.2g	8%
Dietary Fiber 3.2g	11%
Total Sugars 5.7g	
Protein 4.1g	
Vitamin D 0mcg	0%
Calcium 24mg	2%
Iron 2mg	11%
Potassium 313mg	7%

*The % Daily Value (DV) tells you how much a nutrient in a food serving contributes to a daily diet. 2,000 calorie a day is used for general nutrition advice.

7. Black Bean Burger

Serves: 4

Ingredients

1 16 oz can black beans, drained and rinsed
¼ cup raw oats
½ red pepper, thinly sliced
3 cloves garlic, minced
½ onion, finely diced
1 tbsp flaxseed powder
1 tbsp chili powder
1 tsp hot sauce
¼ cup, pureed avocado

Directions

1. In a big bowl, mash the beans.

2. Process the onion, red pepper, and garlic in a food processor until chunks are formed. Mix this into the bean mixture.

3. Next, mix in flaxseed powder, spices, and avocado.

4. Stir together well, then mix in the oats.

5. Form into patties. Place on a preheated grill brushed with a little olive oil, then grill for about 10 minutes per side.

6. Serve with a little added avocado on top, if desired.

Nutrition Facts

Servings: 4

Amount per serving

Calories 446

% Daily Value*

Total Fat 3.3g — 4%

Saturated Fat 0.5g — 3%

Cholesterol 0mg — 0%

Sodium 58mg — 3%

Total Carbohydrate 80.2g — 29%

Dietary Fiber 20g — 71%

Total Sugars 4g

Protein 26.6g

Vitamin D 4mcg — 20%

Calcium 171mg — 13%

Iron 7mg — 37%

Potassium 1799mg — 38%

The % Daily Value (DV) tells you how much a nutrient in a food serving contributes to a daily diet. 2,000 calorie a day is used for general nutrition advice.

8. Black Bean Soup

Serves: 6

Ingredients

4 cups cooked black beans
3-4 cups vegetable broth
2 cloves garlic, minced
1 medium onion, diced
14.5 oz can diced tomatoes
1 red bell pepper, diced
1 tsp cumin
1/2 tsp smoked paprika
1/2 tsp dried oregano
1/2 tsp salt

Garnish/Toppings:

Diced avocado
Vegan sour cream
Sliced green onion
Chopped tomato

Hot sauce
Fresh lime juice
Crushed tortilla chips

Directions

1. In a pot over medium heat, fry the onion, garlic and red bell pepper in 1/4 cup water until softened, 5 minutes. Add water as needed to avoid sticking.

2. Add the cumin, smoked paprika, oregano, and salt and fry another minute until the spices are fragrant.

3. Add tomatoes, black beans, and vegetable broth. Bring to a boil. Lower heat to medium-low and simmer 15 minutes.

4. Using a blender, puree the soup as you like.

5. Serve hot with the toppings of your choice.

Nutrition Facts

Servings: 6

Amount per serving

Calories 492

% Daily Value*

Total Fat 2.7g	3%
Saturated Fat 0.7g	3%
Cholesterol 0mg	0%
Sodium 730mg	32%
Total Carbohydrate 88.5g	32%
Dietary Fiber 21.7g	77%
Total Sugars 7.3g	
Protein 31.5g	
Vitamin D 0mcg	0%
Calcium 189mg	15%
Iron 7mg	41%
Potassium 2102mg	45%

*The % Daily Value (DV) tells you how much a nutrient in a food serving contributes to a daily diet. 2,000 calorie a day is used for general nutrition advice.

9. Buckwheat Salad

Serves: 2

Ingredients

¼ cup olive oil
1 cup raw buckwheat
1 ripe avocado
½ red onion finely chopped
2 spring onions chopped
2 handfuls baby spinach
1 handful fresh basil leaves
juice of a ½ lemon
zest of 1 lemon
2 tbsp pepitas
2 tbsp mixed sprouts
1 fresh red chili thinly sliced
sea salt and pepper to taste

Directions

1. Wash the buckwheat under cold water then boil in a pot with 2 cups of water.

2. Reduce the heat and let it simmer for 15 minutes or until soft. Meanwhile, the buckwheat is cooking mix the baby spinach, basil, spring onions, lemon zest and lemon juice in a food processor and process until chopped.

3. When the buckwheat is cooked let it cool then mix in the herb mixture. Add the red onion and season with salt and pepper.

4. Arrange the buckwheat on a platter, drizzle with olive oil, scatter the chopped chili and sprouts over the top and put the sliced avocado.

Nutrition Facts

Servings: 2

Amount per serving

Calories   684

% Daily Value*

Total Fat 53.6g	**69%**
Saturated Fat 12.2g	**61%**
Cholesterol 25mg	**8%**
Sodium 405mg	**18%**
Total Carbohydrate 43.4g	**16%**
Dietary Fiber 15.7g	**56%**
Total Sugars 5.2g	
Protein 14.3g	
Vitamin D 0mcg	0%
Calcium 200mg	15%
Iron 3mg	17%
Potassium 611mg	13%

*The % Daily Value (DV) tells you how much a nutrient in a food serving contributes to a daily diet. 2,000 calorie a day is used for general nutrition advice.

10. Thai Quinoa Salad

Serves: 2

Ingredients

For Dressing:

    ½ tsp. toasted sesame oil
    ¼ cup tahini
    1 pitted date
    2 tsp. tamari
    1 tbsp. sesame seeds
    3 tsp. apple cider vinegar
    1 tsp. chopped garlic
    1 tsp. lemon, fresh juiced
    ½ Tsp. salt

For Salad:

    1 cup of quinoa, steamed
    ¼ red onion, diced

1 large handful of arugula
1 tomato, sliced

Directions

1. In a blender, add the following: ¼ cup + 2 tbsp. filtered water and the rest of the ingredients. Blend.
2. Steam 1 cup of quinoa in a steamer or rice cooker, then keep aside. Mix, quinoa, arugula, sliced tomatoes, diced red onion, in a bowl, add Thai dressing, and hand mix with a spoon and serve.

Nutrition Facts

Servings: 2

Amount per serving

Calories 558

% Daily Value*

Total Fat 24.8g	32%
Saturated Fat 3.3g	17%
Cholesterol 0mg	0%
Sodium 959mg	42%
Total Carbohydrate 68.7g	25%
Dietary Fiber 10.4g	37%
Total Sugars 4.4g	
Protein 19.2g	
Vitamin D 0mcg	0%
Calcium 226mg	17%
Iron 8mg	42%
Potassium 775mg	16%

*The % Daily Value (DV) tells you how much a nutrient in a food serving contributes to a daily diet. 2,000 calorie a day is used for general nutrition advice.

11. Waldorf Salad

Serves: 4

Ingredients

   2 cups cooked chickpeas
   1-2 apples, chopped
   1 ripe avocado
   1/2 red onion, diced
   1 stalk celery, diced
   Juice of 1/2 lemon
   1-2 teaspoons fresh dill, chopped
   1 cup soaked sunflower seeds
   1 teaspoon Dijon mustard
   sea salt
   fresh cracked pepper to taste

Directions

1. Soak sunflower seeds overnight.

2. Cook chickpeas in advance and refrigerate.
3. Prepare onion, celery, and apple.
4. Using a bowl, mix lemon juice, avocado, Dijon mustard, sea salt, and pepper. Mash nicely using a fork.
5. Mix together chickpeas, sunflower seeds, and mashed avocado mix until well mixed.
6. Top with a little fresh dill and serve.

Nutrition Facts

Servings: 4

Amount per serving
Calories 927

	% Daily Value*
Total Fat 53.1g	**68%**
Saturated Fat 5.9g	**30%**
Cholesterol 0mg	**0%**
Sodium 170mg	**7%**
Total Carbohydrate 89.6g	**33%**
Dietary Fiber 28.9g	**103%**
Total Sugars 20g	
Protein 35.7g	
Vitamin D 0mcg	0%
Calcium 180mg	14%
Iron 11mg	61%
Potassium 1698mg	36%

*The % Daily Value (DV) tells you how much a nutrient in a food serving contributes to a daily diet. 2,000 calorie a day is used for general nutrition advice.

12. Hearty Soup

Serves: 4

Ingredients

   3 tbsp coconut oil
   6 cups vegetable stock
   15 oz. white beans

2 carrots
3 leeks, sliced
1 fennel, sliced
4 rosemary sprigs, leaves chopped
4 garlic cloves, minced
1 cup cabbage, sliced
Some parsley, chopped
Sea salt and pepper to taste

Directions

1. In a pot, heat the oil over medium heat and add carrots, leeks, and fennel. Cook until leeks are tender.
2. Add rosemary, cabbage, and garlic. Cook for 2 minutes.
3. Pour in the stock and bring to a boil.
4. Add the beans and cook for 10 minutes or until tender.
5. Mix in parsley, salt, and pepper. Enjoy!

Nutrition Facts

Servings: 4

Amount per serving

Calories 529

	% Daily Value*
Total Fat 12.2g	**16%**
Saturated Fat 9.7g	**48%**
Cholesterol 0mg	**0%**
Sodium 267mg	**12%**
Total Carbohydrate 84.1g	**31%**
Dietary Fiber 21g	**75%**
Total Sugars 7.4g	
Protein 27.3g	
Vitamin D 0mcg	0%
Calcium 362mg	28%
Iron 14mg	76%
Potassium 2427mg	52%

*The % Daily Value (DV) tells you how much a nutrient in a food serving contributes to a daily diet. 2,000 calorie a day is used for general nutrition advice.

13. Cream of Asparagus Soup

Serves: 4

Ingredients

2 tbsp olive
5 cups vegetable broth
2 lb. asparagus, cut into pieces
1 onion, chopped
1 garlic clove, chopped
Sea salt and pepper to taste
Lemon juice to taste

Directions

1. In a pot, heat the oil over medium heat.

2. Add asparagus, pepper, and salt. Cook for 2 minutes, stirring often.

3. Add broth and bring to a boil and, then simmer for 15 minutes.

4. Blend in a blender and serve with a squeeze of lemon juice.

Nutrition Facts

Servings: 4

Amount per serving

Calories 110

	% Daily Value*
Total Fat 2.5g	3%
Saturated Fat 0.6g	3%
Cholesterol 0mg	0%
Sodium 996mg	43%
Total Carbohydrate 13g	5%
Dietary Fiber 5.5g	20%
Total Sugars 6.3g	
Protein 11.4g	
Vitamin D 0mcg	0%
Calcium 78mg	6%
Iron 6mg	32%
Potassium 760mg	16%

*The % Daily Value (DV) tells you how much a nutrient in a food serving contributes to a daily diet. 2,000 calorie a day is used for general nutrition advice.

14. Greens Lentil Soup

Serves: 4

Ingredients

- 1 tbsp olive oil
- 5 cups water
- 1 cup lentils, dried
- 14 oz tomatoes, crushed
- ½ onion
- 1 carrot, diced
- 1 garlic clove, minced
- 1 celery stalk, diced
- 1 tsp dried oregano
- 1 bay leaf
- ½ cup fresh greens
- 1 lemon, juiced
- Salt and pepper to taste

Directions

1. In a pan, heat the oil and sauté onion, celery, and carrot until soft.
2. Add the herbs and garlic. Stir for 2 minutes and lentils, tomatoes, and water.
3. Bring to a boil and, then simmer for 25 minutes.
4. Add greens and season with salt, lemon juice, and pepper. Enjoy!

Nutrition Facts

Servings: 4

Amount per serving

Calories 239

% Daily Value*

Total Fat 4.3g | **6%**
Saturated Fat 0.6g | **3%**
Cholesterol 0mg | **0%**
Sodium 34mg | **1%**
Total Carbohydrate 38.1g | **14%**
Dietary Fiber 17.4g | **62%**
Total Sugars 5.4g
Protein 13.9g

Vitamin D 0mcg | 0%
Calcium 81mg | 6%
Iron 4mg | 24%
Potassium 827mg | 18%

The % Daily Value (DV) tells you how much a nutrient in a food serving contributes to a daily diet. 2,000 calorie a day is used for general nutrition advice.

15. Pumpkin Soup

Serves: 6

Ingredients

- 2 ½ cups of water
- 2 vegetable bouillon
- 2 cups cauliflower florets
- ½ cup sweet onion
- 3 cups baby spinach
- 1 tsp garlic powder
- 15 oz pumpkin puree
- 15 oz white beans
- 1 tbsp tarragon, dried

Directions

1. In an instant pot, add all the ingredients except spinach. Cook over high heat for 5 minutes.
2. Release the heat and mix in spinach. Cover for 5 minutes and serve.

Nutrition Facts

Servings: 6

Amount per serving
Calories 281

	% Daily Value*
Total Fat 1.1g	1%
Saturated Fat 0.4g	2%
Cholesterol 0mg	0%
Sodium 178mg	8%
Total Carbohydrate 52.3g	19%
Dietary Fiber 14.3g	**51%**
Total Sugars 5.2g	
Protein 18.7g	
Vitamin D 0mcg	0%
Calcium 220mg	17%
Iron 9mg	50%
Potassium 1632mg	35%

The % Daily Value (DV) tells you how much a nutrient in a food serving contributes to a daily diet. 2,000 calorie a day is used for general nutrition advice.

16. Barbecue Tofu

Serves: 4

Ingredients

2 containers tofu
1 1/2 cups ketchup
1 tbsp apple cider vinegar
2 tbsp soy sauce
3 tbsp of brown sugar
1 tbsp red pepper flakes (use a bit less if you're cooking for kids)
1/2 tsp garlic powder
Kosher salt and ground black pepper to taste

Directions

1. Press your tofu.

2. When the tofu is well-pressed, cut it into chunks, and mix the tofu with the remaining ingredients in a crock pot.

3. Cover and cook on low for 5 hours.

4. Serve and enjoy!

Nutrition Facts

Servings: 4

Amount per serving

Calories 212

% Daily Value*

Total Fat 5.8g	7%
Saturated Fat 1.2g	6%
Cholesterol 0mg	0%
Sodium 1471mg	64%
Total Carbohydrate 33g	12%
Dietary Fiber 1.9g	7%
Total Sugars 28.2g	
Protein 12.6g	
Vitamin D 0mcg	0%
Calcium 279mg	21%
Iron 3mg	16%
Potassium 590mg	13%

*The % Daily Value (DV) tells you how much a nutrient in a food serving contributes to a daily diet. 2,000 calorie a day is used for general nutrition advice.

Snacks

1. Protein Queso

Serves: 2

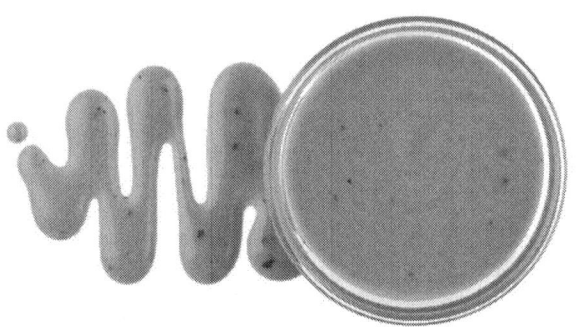

Ingredients

½ block tofu
3 tbsp lemon juice
¼ cup nutritional yeast
½ tsp salt
¼ tsp turmeric powder
¼ tsp cornstarch
¼ tsp of garlic powder
¼ tsp of onion powder
¼ cup of water

Directions

1. Blend tofu, lemon juice, yeast, turmeric, salt, cornstarch, garlic powder, and onion powder in a blender until smooth.
2. Add water if needed to reach the desired thickness.

3. Heat in the oven for 30 seconds and serve with chips of your choice.

Nutrition Facts

Servings: 2

Amount per serving
Calories 95

	% Daily Value*
Total Fat 2.2g	3%
Saturated Fat 0.5g	3%
Cholesterol 0mg	0%
Sodium 602mg	26%
Total Carbohydrate 11g	4%
Dietary Fiber 5.4g	**19%**
Total Sugars 0.8g	
Protein 11.1g	
Vitamin D 0mcg	0%
Calcium 61mg	5%
Iron 4mg	25%
Potassium 553mg	12%

*The % Daily Value (DV) tells you how much a nutrient in a food serving contributes to a daily diet. 2,000 calorie a day is used for general nutrition advice.

2. Edamame Spinach Vegan Hummus

Serves: 2

Ingredients

1 cup spinach
1 cup edamame
2 tbsp tahini
3 tbsp lemon juice
1 tsp agave nectar
1 tbsp nutritional yeast
½ tsp garlic powder
½ tsp onion powder
¼ tsp salt

Directions

1. In a blender, blend all the ingredients until smooth.
2. Serve and enjoy!

Nutrition Facts

Servings: 2

Amount per serving
Calories 308

	% Daily Value*
Total Fat 17.3g	22%
Saturated Fat 2.4g	12%
Cholesterol 0mg	0%
Sodium 347mg	15%
Total Carbohydrate 21.6g	8%
Dietary Fiber 8.6g	31%
Total Sugars 1g	
Protein 22.2g	
Vitamin D 0mcg	0%
Calcium 339mg	26%
Iron 7mg	41%
Potassium 1101mg	23%

*The % Daily Value (DV) tells you how much a nutrient in a food serving contributes to a daily diet. 2,000 calorie a day is used for general nutrition advice.

3. Peanut Butter Protein Bars

Serves: 6

Ingredients

1 cup peanut butter
1 ½ cups instant oats
¾ cup honey
1 cup of protein powder

Directions

1. Lina a baking sheet with parchment paper and in a microwave-safe bowl, heat the peanut butter for 30 seconds.
2. Now, mix in oats and protein powder and stir well.
3. Keep in the fridge, covered, for 1 hour.
4. Remove from the fridge and cut in slices. Enjoy!

Nutrition Facts

Servings: 6

Amount per serving

Calories 423

% Daily Value*

Total Fat 22.5g — 29%

Saturated Fat 4.8g — 24%

Cholesterol 0mg — 0%

Sodium 202mg — 9%

Total Carbohydrate 50.5g — 18%

Dietary Fiber 3.7g — 13%

Total Sugars 39g

Protein 12.4g

Vitamin D 0mcg — 0%

Calcium 9mg — 1%

Iron 5mg — 26%

Potassium 342mg — 7%

The % Daily Value (DV) tells you how much a nutrient in a food serving contributes to a daily diet. 2,000 calorie a day is used for general nutrition advice.

4. Chickpea Brownies

Serves: 8

Ingredients

15 oz can chickpeas, drained
60g vegan dark chocolate bar, broken into chunks
1/3 cup cacao
2/3 cup peanut butter
1/3 cup agave
1 tbsp chocolate extract
1/2 teaspoon baking soda
1/2 teaspoon baking powder
Sea salt flakes

Directions

1. Preheat the oven to 350F.
2. Put all of the ingredients, except the dark chocolate chunks, in a blender and blend until smooth.
3. Transfer the ingredients into a bowl. Mix in the dark chocolate chunks.
4. Line a baking pan with parchment paper and add the batter. Spread the batter into the baking dish and if desired, sprinkle sea salt on top.
5. Bake for 20 minutes until you can insert a toothpick and it comes out.
6. Let the brownies cool before removing from the pan and slicing. Enjoy!

Nutrition Facts

Servings: 8

Amount per serving

Calories 265

% Daily Value*

Total Fat 14.4g | 18%

  Saturated Fat 3.8g | 19%

Cholesterol 0mg | 0%

Sodium 365mg | 16%

Total Carbohydrate 31g | 11%

  Dietary Fiber 7.4g | 26%

  Total Sugars 9.7g

Protein 11.2g

Vitamin D 0mcg | 0%

Calcium 41mg | 3%

Iron 4mg | 22%

Potassium 268mg | 6%

The % Daily Value (DV) tells you how much a nutrient in a food serving contributes to a daily diet. 2,000 calorie a day is used for general nutrition advice.

5. Keto Crackers

Serves: 6

Ingredients

- 1 cup of warm water
- 2 cups milled flaxseed
- 1 teaspoon onion powder
- 1 teaspoon garlic powder
- 2 teaspoons sea salt
- 2 tablespoons sesame seeds

Directions

1. Preheat the oven to 350 F.
2. In a bowl, stir together all of the ingredients, except the sesame seeds. Let it set in the bowl for 5 minutes to thicken.
3. Line a baking sheet with parchment paper, then spread out the dough using a spatula until it is thin.
4. Flatten the dough using a roller or spatula, then scatter the sesame seeds on top. Pat them down into the batter.
5. Slice the dough and bake for 45 minutes, until the edges are golden.
6. Let the dough completely cool to room temperature and enjoy.
7. Season sea salt & pepper, and enjoy.

Nutrition Facts

Servings: 6

Amount per serving

Calories   180

	% Daily Value*
Total Fat 14.8g	19%
Saturated Fat 0.2g	1%
Cholesterol 0mg	0%
Sodium 626mg	27%
Total Carbohydrate 12g	4%
Dietary Fiber 11.1g	40%
Total Sugars 0.3g	
Protein 8.7g	
Vitamin D 0mcg	0%
Calcium 86mg	7%
Iron 2mg	13%
Potassium 325mg	7%

*The % Daily Value (DV) tells you how much a nutrient in a food serving contributes to a daily diet. 2,000 calorie a day is used for general nutrition advice.

6. Baked Sweet Potato Shoestring

Serves: 4

Ingredients

3 sweet potatoes
2 tbsp olive oil
Chipotle rub
1 tbsp smoked paprika
1 tsp chili powder
1 tsp black pepper
1/2 tsp cumin
1/2 tsp cayenne
Sea salt to taste

Directions

1. Preheat oven to 420F.
2. Wash the sweet potatoes, then spiralize into noodles.

3. Pat the noodles dry with a paper towel.
4. Place the noodles in a bowl and add the olive oil and seasonings. Mix in a pinch of sea salt, then mix the noodles in the seasoning.
5. Spread on a baking tray lined with parchment paper.
6. Bake for 15 minutes, then begins looking at the potatoes to remove any burned pieces every 5 minutes, until baked. This can take 30 minutes.
7. Season to taste with salt!

Nutrition Facts

Servings: 4

Amount per serving

Calories 169

% Daily Value*

Total Fat 7.5g — 10%

   Saturated Fat 1.1g — 5%

Cholesterol 0mg — 0%

Sodium 148mg — 6%

Total Carbohydrate 26.7g — 10%

   Dietary Fiber 4.1g — 15%

   Total Sugars 5.5g

Protein 2g

Vitamin D 0mcg — 0%

Calcium 25mg — 2%

Iron 1mg — 6%

Potassium 69mg — 1%

*The % Daily Value (DV) tells you how much a nutrient in a food serving contributes to a daily diet. 2,000 calorie a day is used for general nutrition advice.

7. Fruit Salad

Serves: 8

Ingredients

Dressing:

Juice from 3 limes
Juice from 2 oranges
2 tsp arrowroot mixed with 1 tbsp water
1 tbsp honey

Salad:

24 oz watermelon, cut into chunks
10 oz pineapple, cut into chunks
10 oz mango, cut into chunks
6 oz blackberries1-pint blueberries
1 cucumber, peeled and cut into chunks

½ cup chopped mint
1 jalapeno, chopped and seeds removed
Salt to taste

Directions

1. Squeeze limes and oranges into a small bowl and stir in honey.
2. Set a nonstick pan on medium heat and when hot, pour in the sauce.
3. Bring it to a simmer, then mix in the arrowroot starch. Mix immediately and remove from the heat to let it cool, about 7 minutes.
4. Put all the ingredients for the salad in a big bowl and mix everything.
5. Pour in the dressing and gently mix the fruits and veggies in the sauce.
6. Season to taste with salt.

Nutrition Facts

Servings: 8

Amount per serving
Calories   132

% Daily Value*

Total Fat 0.7g	1%
Saturated Fat 0.1g	1%
Cholesterol 0mg	0%
Sodium 6mg	0%
Total Carbohydrate 33.3g	12%
Dietary Fiber 4.5g	16%
Total Sugars 23.6g	
Protein 2.3g	
Vitamin D 0mcg	0%
Calcium 41mg	3%
Iron 2mg	12%
Potassium 393mg	8%

*The % Daily Value (DV) tells you how much a nutrient in a food serving contributes to a daily diet. 2,000 calorie a day is used for general nutrition advice.

8. Candied Carrots

Serves: 4

Ingredients

- 1 tbsp olive oil
- 6 orange carrots
- 5 small purple carrots
- 2 tbsp maple syrup
- 2 tsp cinnamon
- 2 tsp thyme
- 1 scoop of protein powder
- Sea salt & pepper to taste

Directions

1. Preheat the oven to 450F.
2. Slice carrots to make two thin pieces. Place in a bowl.

3. Add olive oil, thyme, 1 tbsp maple syrup, cinnamon, protein powder, and sea salt & pepper.
4. mix the slices in the spices, then put them on a baking sheet with parchment paper.
5. Roast in the oven for 10 minutes, or until the edges are brown.
6. Pour the remaining syrup over the carrots and serve.

Nutrition Facts

Servings: 4

Amount per serving
Calories 147

% Daily Value*

Total Fat 4g	**5%**
Saturated Fat 0.7g	**4%**
Cholesterol 16mg	**5%**
Sodium 110mg	**5%**
Total Carbohydrate 22.4g	**8%**
Dietary Fiber 4.2g	**15%**
Total Sugars 13g	
Protein 6.8g	
Vitamin D 0mcg	0%
Calcium 98mg	8%
Iron 1mg	8%
Potassium 513mg	11%

The % Daily Value (DV) tells you how much a nutrient in a food serving contributes to a daily diet. 2,000 calorie a day is used for general nutrition advice.

9. Plantains With Maple Syrup

Serves: 5

Ingredients

1/4 cup coconut oil
3 ripe plantains
1/2 cup maple syrup
1 tbsp cinnamon
1 scoop of protein powder

Directions

1. Cut the stems off a plantain and peel it. Slice it into pieces.
2. Add coconut oil to a skillet and set it over medium heat. When the skillet is hot, mix in the plantain pieces.
3. Cover and cook for 7 minutes on medium heat.

4. Flip the plantains, then let them cook for another 2 minutes.

5. Add maple syrup, protein powder, then sprinkle on some cinnamon. Mix the plantain pieces together to ensure they are evenly coated.

6. Let the plantains cool, then enjoy!

Nutrition Facts

Servings: 5

Amount per serving
Calories   335

	% Daily Value*
Total Fat 11.8g	**15%**
Saturated Fat 9.8g	**49%**
Cholesterol 13mg	**4%**
Sodium 18mg	**1%**
Total Carbohydrate 57.2g	**21%**
Dietary Fiber 3.2g	**11%**
Total Sugars 35.1g	
Protein 5.9g	
Vitamin D 0mcg	0%
Calcium 58mg	4%
Iron 1mg	7%
Potassium 641mg	14%

*The % Daily Value (DV) tells you how much a nutrient in a food serving contributes to a daily diet. 2,000 calorie a day is used for general nutrition advice.

10. Roasted Chickpeas

Serves: 4

Ingredients

2 tbsp olive oil
1 can of chickpeas, drained
1 tbsp harissa spice blend
1 pinch of salt

Directions

1. Heat your oven to 450 degrees.
2. In a bowl, mix the chickpeas and spices together until the beans are coated.
3. Put in the oven for 40 minutes on a baking sheet. Enjoy.

Nutrition Facts

Servings: 4

Amount per serving
Calories   424

% Daily Value*

Total Fat 13g   17%

  Saturated Fat 1.6g   8%

Cholesterol 0mg   0%

Sodium 24mg   1%

Total Carbohydrate 60.7g   22%

  Dietary Fiber 17.4g   **62%**

  Total Sugars 10.7g

Protein 19.3g

Vitamin D 0mcg   0%

Calcium 105mg   8%

Iron 6mg   35%

Potassium 875mg   19%

*The % Daily Value (DV) tells you how much a nutrient in a food serving contributes to a daily diet. 2,000 calorie a day is used for general nutrition

11. Trail Mix

Serves: 1

Ingredients

- 1 tbsp sunflower seeds
- 1 tbsp pumpkin seeds
- 1 tbsp almonds
- 1 tbsp hazelnuts
- 1 tbsp currants
- 1 tbsp sultanas

Directions

1. Roast seeds in a pan until golden brown.
2. Roast nuts in a pan until golden brown.
3. Mix all ingredients and enjoy!

Nutrition Facts

Servings: 1

Amount per serving

Calories   138

	% Daily Value*
Total Fat 11.3g	14%
Saturated Fat 1.3g	7%
Cholesterol 0mg	0%
Sodium 2mg	0%
Total Carbohydrate 6.8g	2%
Dietary Fiber 2.1g	8%
Total Sugars 2.6g	
Protein 4.8g	

Vitamin D 0mcg	0%
Calcium 31mg	2%
Iron 2mg	11%
Potassium 201mg	4%

*The % Daily Value (DV) tells you how much a nutrient in a food serving contributes to a daily diet. 2,000 calorie a day is used for general nutrition advice.

12. Butter Bean Dip

Serves: 2

Ingredients

1 tbsp olive oil
1 cup butter beans, cooked
2 tbsp lemon Juice
2 cloves garlic, chopped
1/2 onion, chopped
1/4 cup fresh parsley
Salt to taste

Directions

1. In a bowl, mash butter beans until creamy. Add remaining ingredients.
2. Mix together until well-blended.
3. Adjust seasoning to taste.

4. Transfer into a bowl and garnish with olives.
5. Serve with vegetables or whole meal crackers.

Nutrition Facts

Servings: 2

Amount per serving

Calories 170

% Daily Value*

Total Fat 7.9g	10%
Saturated Fat 1.3g	6%
Cholesterol 0mg	0%
Sodium 15mg	1%
Total Carbohydrate 20.1g	7%
Dietary Fiber 4.8g	17%
Total Sugars 2.7g	
Protein 6.2g	
Vitamin D 0mcg	0%
Calcium 50mg	4%
Iron 3mg	17%
Potassium 477mg	10%

*The % Daily Value (DV) tells you how much a nutrient in a food serving contributes to a daily diet. 2,000 calorie a day is used for general nutrition advice.

13. Maple Glazed Pecans

Serves: 2

Ingredients

 1 tbsp coconut oil
 1 cup raw pecans
 2 tbsp maple syrup
 Pinch of sea salt
 ½ teaspoon of ground cinnamon

Directions

1. Add pecans to a frying pan and toast until browned for 3-4 minutes.
2. Turn flame to low, add the coconut oil, maple syrup and salt and stir for another 2 minutes, until the maple syrup has caramelized the pecans.

3. Leave in pan for a few minutes.
4. Spread the pecans out on a large plate.
5. Let cool completely and enjoy!

Nutrition Facts

Servings: 2

Amount per serving
Calories 216

	% Daily Value*
Total Fat 17.7g	23%
Saturated Fat 6.8g	34%
Cholesterol 0mg	0%
Sodium 119mg	5%
Total Carbohydrate 15.9g	6%
Dietary Fiber 1.8g	6%
Total Sugars 12.4g	
Protein 1.5g	
Vitamin D 0mcg	0%
Calcium 39mg	3%
Iron 1mg	6%
Potassium 43mg	1%

*The % Daily Value (DV) tells you how much a nutrient in a food serving contributes to a daily diet. 2,000 calorie a day is used for general nutrition advice.

14. Chickpea Cookie Dough

Serves: 4

Ingredients

1 cup chickpeas, skins removed
2 tablespoons agave nectar
1/3 cup natural peanut butter
1/3 cup vegan chocolate chips
1 1/2 teaspoons vanilla extract

Directions

1. Mix chickpeas, vanilla extract, peanut butter, and agave in a blender. Blend until pureed.
2. Remove cookie dough mixture from the blender, and transfer in a bowl. Add vegan chocolate chips, and mix well with a spoon. Enjoy!

Nutrition Facts

Servings: 4

Amount per serving

Calories   377

% Daily Value*

Total Fat 15g	**19%**
Saturated Fat 3g	**15%**
Cholesterol 0mg	**0%**
Sodium 19mg	**1%**
Total Carbohydrate 45.9g	**17%**
Dietary Fiber 10.4g	**37%**
Total Sugars 17.9g	
Protein 16.7g	
Vitamin D 0mcg	0%
Calcium 53mg	4%
Iron 6mg	35%
Potassium 440mg	9%

*The % Daily Value (DV) tells you how much a nutrient in a food serving contributes to a daily diet. 2,000 calorie a day is used for general nutrition advice.

15. Roasted Edamame

Serves: 4

Ingredients

2 tsp olive oil
2 cups shelled edamame, thawed
1 tsp sea salt
1 tbsp black sesame seeds

Directions

1. Preheat your oven to 450°F.

2. In a big bowl, mix the edamame with the oil and season with salt.

3. Transfer the edamame to a baking sheet. Bake for almost 15 minutes.

4. Remove from the oven and sprinkle with the sesame seeds.

5. Put back in the oven and bake an additional 5 minutes.

Nutrition Facts

Servings: 4

Amount per serving

Calories   **122**

	% Daily Value*
Total Fat 7.2g	9%
Saturated Fat 0.8g	4%
Cholesterol 0mg	0%
Sodium 476mg	21%
Total Carbohydrate 7.2g	3%
Dietary Fiber 2.5g	9%
Total Sugars 1.5g	
Protein 7.9g	
Vitamin D 0mcg	0%
Calcium 97mg	7%
Iron 2mg	9%
Potassium 354mg	8%

*The % Daily Value (DV) tells you how much a nutrient in a food serving contributes to a daily diet. 2,000 calorie a day is used for general nutrition advice.

16. Tofu Nuggets

Serves: 4

Ingredientes

   3 tbsp vegetable oil
   1/3 cup soy milk
   1 block tofu
   2 tbsp mustard
   1 tbsp nutritional yeast
   1 tsp garlic powder
   1 tsp onion powder
   1 tsp parsley, dried
   1/4 tsp black pepper
   1/2 tsp sea salt
   1/2 cup panko breadcrumbs

Directions

1. Slice the tofu into 1-inch cubes.

2. In a bowl, mix together the soy milk, nutritional yeast, mustard, and spices until smooth.

3. Mix together soy and nutritional yeast.

4. Place the panko breadcrumbs in another bowl.

5. Heat the oil in a pan on medium heat.

6. Take the piece of tofu and dip it in the liquid mixture. Then dip it in the breadcrumbs until well coated.

7. Add it to the pan and repeat the process.

8. Fry the tofu pieces, turning often, until golden brown.

9. Serve and enjoy!

Nutrition Facts

Servings: 4

Amount per serving

Calories 166

% Daily Value*

Total Fat 13.3g	17%
Saturated Fat 2.3g	12%
Cholesterol 0mg	0%
Sodium 267mg	12%
Total Carbohydrate 7.7g	3%
Dietary Fiber 2.2g	8%
Total Sugars 1.8g	
Protein 5.5g	
Vitamin D 0mcg	0%
Calcium 86mg	7%
Iron 2mg	10%
Potassium 173mg	4%

*The % Daily Value (DV) tells you how much a nutrient in a food serving contributes to a daily diet. 2,000 calorie a day is used for general nutrition advice.

Shakes and Smoothies

1. Almond Banana Cream Shake

Serves: 1

Ingredients

½ cup skim milk
1 banana
10 almonds
½ scoop pea protein powder
½ scoop brown rice powder
Ice

Directions

1. In a blender, blend all the ingredients until smooth. Enjoy!

Nutrition Facts

Servings: 1

Amount per serving

Calories 314

% Daily Value*

Total Fat 7.9g	**10%**
Saturated Fat 0.6g	**3%**
Cholesterol 2mg	**1%**
Sodium 256mg	**11%**
Total Carbohydrate 37.5g	**14%**
Dietary Fiber 5.1g	**18%**
Total Sugars 20.9g	
Protein 27.8g	
Vitamin D 1mcg	3%
Calcium 238mg	18%
Iron 6mg	32%
Potassium 700mg	15%

*The % Daily Value (DV) tells you how much a nutrient in a food serving contributes to a daily diet. 2,000 calorie a day is used for general nutrition advice.

2. Coconut Cream Pie Protein Shake

Serves: 1

Ingredients

1 tbsp coconut oil
1 tbsp coconut cream
1 banana, frozen
¾ cup of coconut milk
1 scoop vanilla protein powder
2 tbsp coconut flakes
Ice

Directions

1. In a blender, blend all the ingredients and enjoy.

Nutrition Facts

Servings: 1

Amount per serving

Calories 799

% Daily Value*

Total Fat 61.2g	**79%**
Saturated Fat 54g	**270%**
Cholesterol 80mg	**27%**
Sodium 180mg	**8%**
Total Carbohydrate 41.4g	**15%**
Dietary Fiber 4.3g	**15%**
Total Sugars 17.6g	
Protein 31.6g	
Vitamin D 0mcg	0%
Calcium 51mg	4%
Iron 10mg	55%
Potassium 1114mg	24%

*The % Daily Value (DV) tells you how much a nutrient in a food serving contributes to a daily diet. 2,000 calorie a day is used for general nutrition advice.

3. Blue Protein Smoothie

Serves: 3

Ingredients

- 2 cups baby spinach
- 1 cup blueberries, frozen
- 1 cup strawberries, frozen
- 2 tbsp maple syrup
- 2 tbsp almond butter
- 3 tbsp hemp seeds
- 1-inch ginger, peeled and chopped
- 1 cup of water

Directions

1. In a blender, blend all the ingredients and enjoy!

Nutrition Facts

Servings: 3

Amount per serving

Calories   234

% Daily Value*

Total Fat 13.3g	17%
Saturated Fat 0.9g	4%
Cholesterol 0mg	0%
Sodium 19mg	1%
Total Carbohydrate 23.8g	9%
Dietary Fiber 4.2g	15%
Total Sugars 15.7g	
Protein 8.6g	
Vitamin D 0mcg	0%
Calcium 51mg	4%
Iron 5mg	30%
Potassium 478mg	10%

*The % Daily Value (DV) tells you how much a nutrient in a food serving contributes to a daily diet. 2,000 calorie a day is used for general nutrition advice.

4. Coconut Strawberry Protein Smoothie

Serves: 2

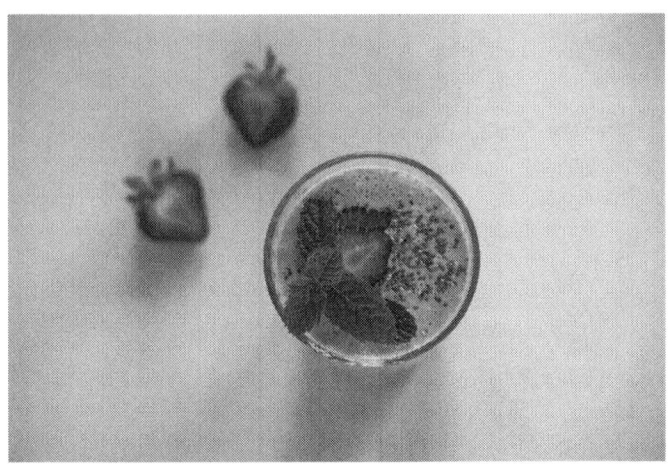

Ingredients

¼ cup vanilla protein powder
1 cup strawberries, frozen
1 cup of coconut milk
2 tsp honey
1 tsp flax seeds, ground
1 tsp vanilla extract

Directions

1. In a blender, blend all the ingredients and enjoy.

Nutrition Facts

Servings: 2

Amount per serving
Calories 370

% Daily Value*

Total Fat 29.7g	**38%**
Saturated Fat 25.7g	**128%**
Cholesterol 20mg	**7%**
Sodium 57mg	**2%**
Total Carbohydrate 20.3g	**7%**
Dietary Fiber 4.4g	**16%**
Total Sugars 14.1g	
Protein 10g	

Vitamin D 0mcg	0%
Calcium 34mg	3%
Iron 3mg	17%
Potassium 497mg	11%

*The % Daily Value (DV) tells you how much a nutrient in a food serving contributes to a daily diet. 2,000 calorie a day is used for general nutrition advice.

5. Peanut Butter Green Smoothie

Serves: 2

Ingredients

1 ½ cups vanilla almond milk
3 dates, pitted
1 tbsp cocoa powder
1 tbsp creamy peanut butter
1 banana, frozen
2 cups spinach, frozen
2 tbsp old fashioned oats
2 cups kale frozen

Directions

1. Put ingredients in a blender.
2. Serve immediately!

Nutrition Facts

Servings: 2

Amount per serving

Calories   248

	% Daily Value*
Total Fat 7.9g	10%
Saturated Fat 1.4g	7%
Cholesterol 0mg	0%
Sodium 501mg	22%
Total Carbohydrate 41.2g	15%
Dietary Fiber 8.8g	31%
Total Sugars 18g	
Protein 10g	
Vitamin D 1mcg	5%
Calcium 563mg	43%
Iron 4mg	25%
Potassium 1160mg	25%

*The % Daily Value (DV) tells you how much a nutrient in a food serving contributes to a daily diet. 2,000 calorie a day is used for general nutrition advice.

6. Peanut Butter Protein Shake

Serves: 1

Ingredients

- 1/4 cup peanut flour
- 1 cup chocolate almond milk
- 2 frozen bananas sliced
- 2 tablespoons chia seeds

Directions

1. Put all ingredients in a blender and blend until smooth.
2. Serve.

Nutrition Facts

Servings: 1

Amount per serving

Calories 450

% Daily Value*

Total Fat 16.6g — 21%

Saturated Fat 1.5g — 8%

Cholesterol 0mg — 0%

Sodium 143mg — 6%

Total Carbohydrate 78.6g — 29%

Dietary Fiber 18.5g — 66%

Total Sugars 34.9g

Protein 14.7g

Vitamin D 100mcg — 500%

Calcium 271mg — 21%

Iron 4mg — 21%

Potassium 1247mg — 27%

*The % Daily Value (DV) tells you how much a nutrient in a food serving contributes to a daily diet. 2,000 calorie a day is used for general nutrition advice.

7. Red Juice

Serves: 2

Ingredients

1 cup kale
1 large beet
2 red apples
2 medium carrots
1-inch ginger

Directions

1. Juice kale.

2. Then juice carrots, apples, beets and ginger. Enjoy!

Nutrition Facts

Servings: 2

Amount per serving

Calories 183

% Daily Value*

Total Fat 0.5g	**1%**
Saturated Fat 0g	**0%**
Cholesterol 0mg	**0%**
Sodium 97mg	**4%**
Total Carbohydrate 45.9g	**17%**
Dietary Fiber 8.5g	**30%**
Total Sugars 30.2g	
Protein 3g	

Vitamin D 0mcg	0%
Calcium 75mg	6%
Iron 2mg	12%
Potassium 763mg	16%

*The % Daily Value (DV) tells you how much a nutrient in a food serving contributes to a daily diet. 2,000 calorie a day is used for general nutrition advice.

8. Nut Smoothie

Serves: 2

Ingredients

- 1 cup of coconut milk
- 1 frozen banana
- 2 tbsp almond butter
- 1 tsp vanilla
- 1 tsp honey
- 1 tbsp cacao

Directions

1. In a blender, blend all the ingredients and enjoy!

Nutrition Facts

Servings: 2

Amount per serving

Calories 468

	% Daily Value*
Total Fat 39.8g	**51%**
Saturated Fat 27.4g	**137%**
Cholesterol 0mg	**0%**
Sodium 20mg	**1%**
Total Carbohydrate 31.3g	**11%**
Dietary Fiber 8.8g	**31%**
Total Sugars 15.1g	
Protein 8.8g	
Vitamin D 0mcg	0%
Calcium 38mg	3%
Iron 6mg	34%
Potassium 652mg	14%

*The % Daily Value (DV) tells you how much a nutrient in a food serving contributes to a daily diet. 2,000 calorie a day is used for general nutrition advice.

9. Pineapple Pie Smoothie

Serves: 2

Ingredients

1 cup pineapple
1/3 cup coconut cream
1 cup of coconut milk
Juice from 2 limes
1 tsp ginger
1 scoop of protein powder
Cinnamon to taste

Directions

1. In a blender, blend all the ingredients and enjoy!

Nutrition Facts

Servings: 2

Amount per serving
Calories   568

% Daily Value*

Total Fat 37.8g	**48%**
Saturated Fat 33.5g	**167%**
Cholesterol 32mg	**11%**
Sodium 66mg	**3%**
Total Carbohydrate 50g	**18%**
Dietary Fiber 4.3g	**15%**
Total Sugars 38.8g	
Protein 15.1g	
Vitamin D 0mcg	0%
Calcium 90mg	7%
Iron 3mg	15%
Potassium 607mg	13%

*The % Daily Value (DV) tells you how much a nutrient in a food serving contributes to a daily diet. 2,000 calorie a day is used for general nutrition advice.

10. Orange Turmeric Smoothie

Serves: 1

Ingredients

- 7 oz coconut yogurt
- 1/2 cup almond milk
- 1 1/2 oranges, peeled
- 1/3 cup cantaloupe
- 2 tsp vanilla extract
- 1/2 teaspoon turmeric

Directions

1. In a blender, blend all the ingredients and enjoy!

Nutrition Facts

Servings: 1

Amount per serving

Calories 487

% Daily Value*

Total Fat 30.8g	**40%**
Saturated Fat 26.7g	**133%**
Cholesterol 0mg	**0%**
Sodium 28mg	**1%**
Total Carbohydrate 49g	**18%**
Dietary Fiber 10g	**36%**
Total Sugars 38.9g	
Protein 7.1g	
Vitamin D 0mcg	0%
Calcium 137mg	11%
Iron 3mg	16%
Potassium 994mg	21%

The % Daily Value (DV) tells you how much a nutrient in a food serving contributes to a daily diet. 2,000 calorie a day is used for general nutrition advice.

11. Mango Lassi

Serves: 1

Ingredients

1¼ cup of coconut yogurt
1 mango
2½ cup of water

Directions

1. Peel, halve and remove the stones from the mango.
2. Blend in a blender with the other ingredients. Enjoy.

Nutrition Facts

Servings: 1

Amount per serving
Calories 339

% Daily Value*

Total Fat 6.2g	8%
Saturated Fat 3.4g	17%
Cholesterol 0mg	0%
Sodium 3mg	0%
Total Carbohydrate 67.5g	25%
Dietary Fiber 5.4g	19%
Total Sugars 62.4g	
Protein 7.6g	
Vitamin D 0mcg	0%
Calcium 37mg	3%
Iron 1mg	3%
Potassium 564mg	12%

*The % Daily Value (DV) tells you how much a nutrient in a food serving contributes to a daily diet. 2,000 calorie a day is used for general nutrition advice.

12. Strawberry Almond Protein Smoothie

Serves: 1

Ingredients

    1 cup frozen strawberries
    1/2 cup almonds, soaked overnight
    2 dates
    1/2 cup water

Directions

1. In a blender, blend all the ingredients and enjoy!

Nutrition Facts

Servings: 1

Amount per serving

Calories 372

% Daily Value*

Total Fat 23.8g	31%
Saturated Fat 1.8g	9%
Cholesterol 0mg	0%
Sodium 1mg	0%
Total Carbohydrate 35.6g	13%
Dietary Fiber 10.3g	37%
Total Sugars 21.5g	
Protein 10.5g	
Vitamin D 0mcg	0%
Calcium 154mg	12%
Iron 3mg	15%
Potassium 457mg	10%

*The % Daily Value (DV) tells you how much a nutrient in a food serving contributes to a daily diet. 2,000 calorie a day is used for general nutrition advice.

13. Banana Orange Smoothie

Serves: 2

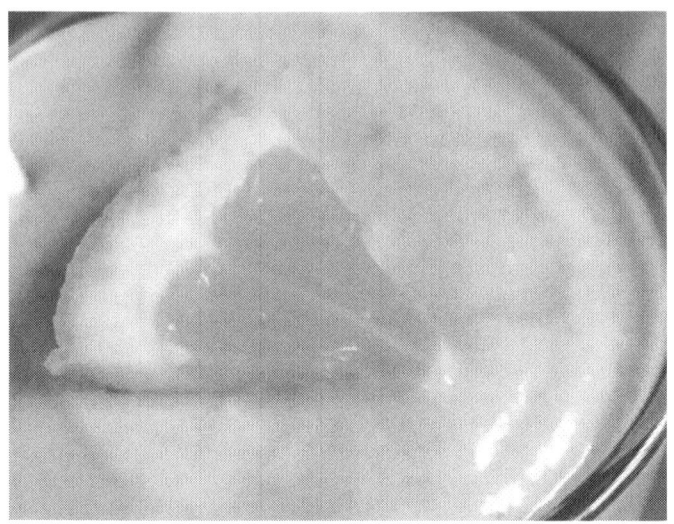

Ingredients

2 frozen bananas, cut into chunks
1 cup of coconut milk
1/2 cup coconut yogurt
1/2 cup of orange juice
1/2 avocado
zest of 1 orange

Directions

1. In a blender, blend all the ingredients and enjoy!

Nutrition Facts

Servings: 2

Amount per serving
Calories 539

% Daily Value*

Total Fat 39.9g	**51%**
Saturated Fat 28.2g	**141%**
Cholesterol 0mg	**0%**
Sodium 23mg	**1%**
Total Carbohydrate 47.8g	**17%**
Dietary Fiber 9.2g	**33%**
Total Sugars 27.2g	
Protein 6.4g	
Vitamin D 0mcg	0%
Calcium 32mg	2%
Iron 3mg	19%
Potassium 1106mg	24%

*The % Daily Value (DV) tells you how much a nutrient in a food serving contributes to a daily diet. 2,000 calorie a day is used for general nutrition advice.

14. Kiwi Smoothie

Serves: 2

Ingredients

- 3 tbsp honey
- 1 cup blueberries
- 3 kiwifruits, peeled and cut into chunks
- 2 bananas, cut into 4 pieces
- 1 cup of coconut yogurt
- 1/4 tsp almond extract

Directions

1. In a blender, blend all the ingredients and enjoy!

Nutrition Facts

Servings: 2

Amount per serving
Calories 434

% Daily Value*

Total Fat 4.1g — 5%

  Saturated Fat 1.4g — 7%

Cholesterol 0mg — 0%

Sodium 3mg — 0%

Total Carbohydrate 100.3g — 36%

  Dietary Fiber 10.9g — 39%

  Total Sugars 73.7g

Protein 5.4g

Vitamin D 0mcg — 0%

Calcium 68mg — 5%

Iron 2mg — 11%

Potassium 495mg — 11%

The % Daily Value (DV) tells you how much a nutrient in a food serving contributes to a daily diet. 2,000 calorie a day is used for general nutrition advice.

15. Pumpkin Protein Smoothie

Serves: 1

Ingredients

- 1 tablespoon almond butter
- 1 1/2 cup homemade almond milk
- 1/2 cup organic pumpkin puree
- 1 scoop vanilla protein powder
- 1/2 teaspoon organic cinnamon powder
- 1/4 teaspoon organic ginger powder
- 1/4 teaspoon organic nutmeg powder

Directions

1. In a blender, blend all the ingredients and enjoy!

Nutrition Facts

Servings: 1

Amount per serving

Calories 379

% Daily Value*

Total Fat 20.3g	26%
Saturated Fat 1.8g	9%
Cholesterol 10mg	3%
Sodium 292mg	13%
Total Carbohydrate 24.5g	9%
Dietary Fiber 5.3g	**19%**
Total Sugars 13.1g	
Protein 30.1g	
Vitamin D 0mcg	0%
Calcium 438mg	34%
Iron 5mg	29%
Potassium 430mg	9%

*The % Daily Value (DV) tells you how much a nutrient in a food serving contributes to a daily diet. 2,000 calorie a day is used for general nutrition advice.

16. Power Packed Smoothie

Serves: 2

Ingredients

1 cup almond milk
1 tablespoon vegan protein powder
2 bananas
1 cup of frozen berries
1/2 cup chopped pineapple

Directions

1. In a blender, blend all the ingredients and enjoy!

Nutrition Facts

Servings: 2

Amount per serving

Calories 497

% Daily Value*

Total Fat 29.8g	**38%**
Saturated Fat 25.5g	**128%**
Cholesterol 0mg	**0%**
Sodium 90mg	**4%**
Total Carbohydrate 50g	**18%**
Dietary Fiber 8.8g	**31%**
Total Sugars 28.5g	
Protein 14.8g	
Vitamin D 0mcg	0%
Calcium 40mg	3%
Iron 3mg	15%
Potassium 873mg	19%

*The % Daily Value (DV) tells you how much a nutrient in a food serving contributes to a daily diet. 2,000 calorie a day is used for general nutrition advice.

17. Chia Lucuma Smoothie

Serves: 2

Ingredients

    1 cup almond milk
    ½ cup of coconut milk

1 cup of water
½ banana
1 tbsp chia seeds
1 tsp cinnamon
2 tsp lucuma powder
½ tsp stevia

Directions

1. In a blender, blend all the ingredients and enjoy!

Nutrition Facts

Servings: 2

Amount per serving

Calories 401

% Daily Value*

Total Fat 33.3g — 43%

Saturated Fat 26g — 130%

Cholesterol 0mg — 0%

Sodium 24mg — 1%

Total Carbohydrate 24.8g — 9%

Dietary Fiber 11.5g — 41%

Total Sugars 8.7g

Protein 5.6g

Vitamin D 0mcg — 0%

Calcium 136mg — 10%

Iron 4mg — 20%

Potassium 477mg — 10%

The % Daily Value (DV) tells you how much a nutrient in a food serving contributes to a daily diet. 2,000 calorie a day is used for general nutrition advice.

18. Tune Up Smoothie

Serves: 1

Ingredients

1 cup water
1 small handful kale
1/4-inch fresh ginger
1/2 cup pineapple, cut into chunks
1 banana
1 tbsp ground chia seed
2 tbsp hemp seeds
1/4 lemon, juiced
1/4 tsp ground turmeric

Directions

1. In a blender, blend all the ingredients and enjoy!

Nutrition Facts

Servings: 1

Amount per serving
Calories 501

% Daily Value*

Total Fat 23.3g	**30%**
Saturated Fat 2g	**10%**
Cholesterol 0mg	**0%**
Sodium 52mg	**2%**
Total Carbohydrate 62.7g	**23%**
Dietary Fiber 18.1g	**65%**
Total Sugars 23g	
Protein 18.5g	

Vitamin D 0mcg	0%
Calcium 343mg	26%
Iron 8mg	47%
Potassium 1252mg	27%

*The % Daily Value (DV) tells you how much a nutrient in a food serving contributes to a daily diet. 2,000 calorie a day is used for general nutrition advice.

19. Mango Hemp Seed Smoothie

Serves: 1

Ingredients

- 1 1/2 cup almond milk
- 1 tbsp organic coconut oil
- 1 scoop of protein powder
- 1 tsp organic vanilla bean powder
- 1 tbsp organic maca powder
- 2 tbsp organic hemp seeds
- 1 tbsp organic lucuma powder
- 1 cup mango
- 2 organic Medrol dates, pitted

Directions

1. In a blender, blend all the ingredients and enjoy!

Nutrition Facts

Servings: 2

Amount per serving

Calories   922

	% Daily Value*
Total Fat 61.2g	**79%**
Saturated Fat 45.2g	**226%**
Cholesterol 45mg	**15%**
Sodium 89mg	**4%**
Total Carbohydrate 68.2g	**25%**
Dietary Fiber 11.8g	**42%**
Total Sugars 47.7g	
Protein 36.4g	
Vitamin D 0mcg	0%
Calcium 478mg	37%
Iron 8mg	43%
Potassium 1007mg	21%

*The % Daily Value (DV) tells you how much a nutrient in a food serving contributes to a daily diet. 2,000 calorie a day is used for general nutrition advice.

20. Spirulina Smoothie

Serves: 1

Ingredients

- 1 cup coconut water
- 1 handful of kale
- 1 banana
- 1 cup pineapple chunks
- 1/2 tsp spirulina
- 1 tsp psyllium husk

Directions

1. In a blender, blend all the ingredients and enjoy!

Nutrition Facts

Servings: 1

Amount per serving

Calories 315

% Daily Value*

Total Fat 1.1g	1%
Saturated Fat 0.6g	3%
Cholesterol 0mg	0%
Sodium 370mg	16%
Total Carbohydrate 78.1g	28%
Dietary Fiber 18.7g	67%
Total Sugars 36.9g	
Protein 8.5g	
Vitamin D 0mcg	0%
Calcium 209mg	16%
Iron 5mg	26%
Potassium 1622mg	35%

*The % Daily Value (DV) tells you how much a nutrient in a food serving contributes to a daily diet. 2,000 calorie a day is used for general nutrition advice.

21. Cashew Milkshake

Serves: 1

Ingredients

1 cup of soy milk
1 banana
3 tbsp cashews
3 tsp cacao powder

Directions

1. In a blender, blend all the ingredients and enjoy!

Nutrition Facts

Servings: 1

Amount per serving

Calories   435

% Daily Value*

Total Fat 20.6g   26%

  Saturated Fat 5.5g   27%

Cholesterol 0mg   0%

Sodium 130mg   6%

Total Carbohydrate 60.8g   22%

  Dietary Fiber 11.3g   40%

  Total Sugars 25.5g

Protein 17.3g

Vitamin D 0mcg   0%

Calcium 99mg   8%

Iron 5mg   29%

Potassium 857mg   18%

*The % Daily Value (DV) tells you how much a nutrient in a food serving contributes to a daily diet. 2,000 calorie a day is used for general nutrition advice.

Manufactured by
Amazon.ca
Bolton, ON